New Directions in British Politics?

New Directions in British Politics?

Essays on the Evolving Constitution

Edited by
Philip Norton
Professor of Government
University of Hull

Edward Elgar

Published by
Edward Elgar Publishing Limited
Gower House
Croft Road
Aldershot
Hants GU11 3HR
England

Edward Elgar Publishing Company
Old Post Road
Brookfield
Vermont 05036
USA

Printed in Great Britain by
Billing & Sons Ltd, Worcester

British Library Cataloguing in Publication Data
New directions in British politics: essays on the evolving
    constitution.
    1. Great Britain. Politics
    I. Norton, Philip
    320.941

Library of Congress Cataloguing in Publication Data
New directions in British politics?: essays on the evolving
    constitution/edited by Philip Norton.
        p. cm.
    Includes bibliographical references and index.
    1. Great Britain–Politics and government–1979– 2. Great
Britain–Constitutional law. I. Norton, Philip.
JN231.N48 1991   90-27737
320.941–dc20   CIP

ISBN 1 85278 350 8

Contents

Preface

All the contributions to this volume, other than my own, were delivered as papers in a seminar series on the theme from which this volume takes its title: New Directions in British Politics. Four of the papers in the series – by Peter Hennessy, Gavin Drewry, Rod Rhodes and Stanley (now Lord) Clinton-Davis – were delivered at the University of Hull under the auspices of Hull University Politics Department; the fifth – by Enoch Powell – was delivered in London under the auspices of the Politics Department's Graduates Association. My own paper on Parliament was delivered at a conference held at the Carl Albert Congressional Research and Studies Centre at the University of Oklahoma. All the papers were delivered in the 1989–90 academic year, but where appropriate have been revised to take into account developments since that time. The chapter on the Constitution was written specifically to conclude the volume.

I am grateful to all the contributors for the time and intellectual effort they invested in delivering stimulating papers and in revising them for publication. My thanks are also owing to Edward Elgar, with whom I originally discussed this project early in 1989, for seeing the work through to publication with his customary care and efficiency.

Each chapter stands as a self-contained contribution to the contemporary debate on the British Constitution. I am responsible for the editorial selection and it is important to stress that I alone am responsible for the views expressed in the concluding chapter.

PHILIP NORTON
University of Hull

Notes on the Contributors

Lord Clinton-Davis was created a Life Peer in 1990. He was a Commissioner of the European Communities, with responsibility for transport, environment and nuclear safety, from 1985 to 1989. Prior to that, he was Labour MP for Hackney Central from 1970 to 1983, serving as Parliamentary Under-Secretary of State for Trade from 1974 to 1979.

Gavin Drewry is Professor of Public Administration at Royal Holloway and Bedford New College, University of London. He is editor of *The New Select Committees* (1985, 2nd edn, 1989) and author or co-author of *Final Appeal* (1972), *Law, Justice and Politics* (1975), *Law and Morality* (1976), *Legislation and Public Policy* (1981) and *The Civil Service Today* (1988).

Peter Hennessy is a journalist, broadcaster and Visiting Professor of Government at the University of Strathclyde. He co-founded the Institute of Contemporary British History. His publications include *Sources Close to the Prime Minister* (joint author, 1984), *What the Papers Never Said* (1985), *Cabinet* (1986), *Ruling Performance* (joint editor, 1987) and *Whitehall* (1989).

Philip Norton is Professor of Government at the University of Hull and a member of the executive committees of the British Politics Group in the USA (President 1988–90) and the Study of Parliament Group. He is the author or editor of more than a dozen books, including *Dissension in the House of Commons* (2 vols, 1975, 1980), *Conservative Dissidents* (1978), *The Commons in Perspective* (1981), *The Constitution in Flux* (1982), *The British Polity* (1984, 2nd edn, 1990), *Parliament in the 1980s* (1985), *Legislatures* (1990) and *Parliaments in Western Europe* (1990).

The Rt Hon. J. Enoch Powell was Conservative MP for Wolverhampton South-West from 1950 to 1974 and Ulster Unionist MP for South

Down from 1974 to 1987. He served as Parliamentary Under-Secretary of State for Housing and Local Government 1955–7, Financial Secretary to the Treasury 1957–8 and Minister of Health 1960–3. He was awarded the MBE (military) in 1943 and became a Privy Counsellor in 1960. His publications include *The House of Lords in the Middle Ages* (with K. Wallis, 1968).

R. A. W. Rhodes is Professor and Head of the Department of Politics at the University of York. His recent publications include *Beyond Westminster* (1988) and *Policy Networks in British Government* (joint editor, 1991). He is the editor of *Public Administration*, the Journal of the Royal Institute of Public Administration.

1. Introduction

Philip Norton

A constitution may be defined as the collectivity of laws, customs and conventions that define the composition and powers of organs of the state and regulate the relations of those organs to one another and to the individual citizen.[1] Britain is distinctive though not unique in that the core provisions of its constitution are not drawn up in a single document; the nation lacks a 'written' constitution. Rather, it has a part-written, uncodified – or what Nevil Johnson has aptly termed an 'unformalised' – constitution.[2] That constitution has, at various times in history, been subject to modification and debate.

Indeed, the constitution in Britain used to be a subject of considerable interest, attracting in the first half of the century the considered reflections of academics such as Harold Laski and politicians such as Leo Amery. Proposals for change came from the pens of Fred Jowett, the Webbs, Winston Churchill, G. D. H. Cole, Ramsay Muir and Stafford Cripps, among others. Lord Hewart's *The New Despotism* (1929) – arguing that the civil service had replaced Parliament as the effective centre of government – caused a particular stir. However, in the years after the Second World War interest waned. As the paragons of prewar years died off, there were no immediate replacements. The constitution ceased to be a subject of both academic and political discourse.

That this should be so is not that surprising. Prewar years had witnessed political and economic upheaval; Laski had written *The Crisis and the Constitution* in response to the events of 1931. Postwar years witnessed political stability and economic recovery, helped in the 1950s by a favourable international economic environment. The country had witnessed the peaceful transfer of power from one party to another and then back again; it manifested the properties of what Sartori was later to characterise as a 'perfect' two-party system.[3] Britain was still a world force, playing a leading role in the United Nations and in the emergence of the British Commonwealth of Nations. There seemed little point in

1

emulating the practices of other, often relatively immature or (worse still) unstable systems of government. The result, as Anthony Lester has noted, was that in the 1950s there was broad satisfaction with our constitutional arrangements.[4]

This sense of satisfaction also appeared to suffuse the academic community. There was little impetus for reflection and debate on the scale that had characterised earlier years. Academic interest turned elsewhere. In so far as the constitution – or, more likely, government – was written about it was for the purposes of description and praise. In the mid-1950s, the student of the constitution had little to draw on other than a work from the pen of a practitioner, Herbert Morrison's *Government and Parliament;* and, a decade later, little other than Harvey and Bather's *The British Constitution.* As Anthony Wright has succinctly commented, Morrison's uncritical – and largely uninsightful – work 'exemplified a mood'.[5] It proved to be relatively short-lived.

Economic downturn and new political uncertainties in the 1960s heralded an era of structural change and, later, debate as to the nature and very future of the constitution. In the first half of the decade, under Harold Macmillan's premiership, there was Britain's first application to join the European Economic Community (the EEC) and a reform of local government in London; in the latter half of the decade, under the Labour government of Harold Wilson, an attempt to reform the House of Lords. The early years of the 1970s witnessed even more radical change, with the Conservative government of Edward Heath embarking on a reorganisation of the National Health Service, local government outside London, and central government departments; and, by force of circumstance, imposing direct rule in Northern Ireland. However, there was little familiarity with discussing the Constitution as such. The approach was that of a mechanic rather than a designer. Parts were variously repaired or modified in order to deal with particular problems. Only as the decade of the 1970s progressed did discussion of the Constitution *qua* Constitution develop and a significant movement for reform of Britain's previously lauded Constitution emerge.

A few pamphlets advocating a Bill of Rights appeared at the end of the 1960s and a book on constitutional reform – O. Hood Phillips's *Reform of the Constitution* – was published in 1970.[6] However, it was to be lectures from two jurists that really sparked debate. Sir Leslie (now Lord) Scarman's Hamlyn Lecture in 1974 and Lord Hailsham's Dimbleby Lecture two years later had a seminal influence.[7] Hailsham's lecture in particular added a new term to the vocabulary of debate: that of an 'elective dictatorship'. Both Scarman and Hailsham looked to a codification of rights enjoying judicial protection. The common-law system, declared Scarman, was in retreat; 'we must seek a new constitutional settlement that makes use of judicial power to keep within constitutional limits the legislative sovereignty of Parliament'.[8] Others began to look to different forms of constitutional change: the latter half of the decade experienced pressure for a new electoral system, based on proportional representation, and an attempt by the Labour government of James Callaghan to devolve power to elected assemblies in Scotland and Wales.[9]

The academic world also began to discover anew the Constitution. In the late 1960s and early 1970s, the emerging discipline of political science had largely reflected and encouraged the managerial reform approach of government.[10] In the late 1970s, as recognition grew that managerial reform by itself was an inadequate tool for solving Britain's problems, works began to address themselves to the Constitution as such. Nevil Johnson's appropriately titled *In Search of the Constitution* (1977) led the way. Others have followed; though still not great in number,[11] such works are certainly more numerous now than in the largely dormant era of the 1950s and early 1960s. Academics are now especially significant contributors to the literature espousing reform.

In the latter half of the 1970s, then, constitutional reform was on the agenda of political debate, championed largely (and consistently) in the political domain, though – as we shall see in Chapter 8 – by no means exclusively, by the Liberal Party. In the 1980s, debate on the constitution waned and then waxed again. For much of the decade the agenda was set by a government intent on using the existing constitutional framework to achieve implementation of a string of radical policy goals. Debate on constitutional reform was largely pushed to the periphery: the concerns of politicians and political scientists were more immediate. However, the changes wrought by government – and both the means and style employed by ministers, and especially the Prime Minister, in order to achieve policy goals – generated renewed interest in the British Constitution.

The Liberal/SDP Alliance made constitutional reform the principal plank of its 1987 election manifesto. The outcome of that election, producing a third consecutive Conservative victory, focused the minds of many on the left. The tercentenary of the Glorious Revolution in 1988 provided further scope for comment and reflection. In that year, Charter '88 – an informal association committed to a new constitutional settlement in Britain, replacing that of 1688–9 – was formed, advancing a daunting menu of constitutional reform. The following year, the fruits of the Labour Party's policy review were published.

In *Meet the Challenge, Make the Change*, Labour's policy review group on 'Democracy for the Individual and the Community' argued for 'a fundamental reform of the institutions which establish and entrench our individual and collective rights': it proposed a new second chamber, devolution of power through the creation of elected assemblies in Scotland and Wales, regional government in England, reform of the House of Commons and state funding of political parties. For the protection of basic liberties, it advocated the introduction of a number of specific measures of legislation, for which the new second chamber would stand as an ultimate protector. 'We propose', declared the document, 'to put individual rights back into the centre of political debate.'[12]

The government for its part has been responsible for a number of measures that have affected the Constitution significantly. Most notable among such measures has been the 1986 European Communities (Amendment) Act, ratifying the Single European Act. Others have included the reform of the structure, operation and financing of local government. Though concern has been expressed by ministers about some of the implications of the Single European Act, the government has not advanced proposals for explicit and radical constitutional surgery: it remains opposed to the concept of a new constitutional settlement. It has stood by the arrangements that have served it well.

The political parties have thus come to adopt very different stances on the issue of constitutional change. In so doing, they are by no means internally united. Proposals for constitutional reform cut across traditional party lines. The result is a lively and not always predictable debate, the political configurations in that debate having changed over time (a point to which I shall return in Chapter 8); the debate has now reached, especially with the formation of Charter '88, a new level of intensity.

The Constitution, then, is a subject of contemporary debate. It has, in effect, been rediscovered by the politician, the public lawyer and the political scientist (or, to be more accurate, by some of those in each of these categories).[13] If the concept of U and non-U can be applied to political debate, the Constitution is very much now a U subject.

The purpose of this volume is to contribute to this growing, but often hazy, debate. It does so through adopting a distinctive approach. That distinctiveness lies both in what it is not as well as in what it seeks to do. It is not a prescriptive text with the contributors being drawn from one particular school of thought and advocating a particular goal. Nor is it comprehensive. It does not cover all aspects of contemporary debate. Rather, it focuses on those topics of debate which, appearances to the contrary notwithstanding, have not been subject to sustained consideration in the burgeoning literature. And within these areas the contributors challenge many of the core tenets on which critiques of the Constitution are based.

Has not Cabinet government in Britain now been finally and irrevocably displaced by Prime Ministerial government? Is not the much-vaunted independence of the judiciary under threat? Is not Parliament incapable, even more so now than before, of influencing government? Has not local government had the life blood sucked from it by a government intent on achieving its grand design for governance? Is not the UK destined to a history of resigned belligerence within the European Community? And, given the centralising tendencies of government – the concentration of power in the hands of the premier, the humbling of local government and other potential challengers – is there not a powerful case for a reformulation of the Constitution, for a new constitutional settlement?

The answers to these questions from those making most of the running in the present debate is, as will be detailed in Chapter 8, a very clear 'yes'. What the contributions to this volume demonstrate is that the situation in each case is not as clear-cut, not as demonstrable, as affirmative answers would imply. The chapters individually and collectively offer a fresh perspective.

PRIME MINISTER AND CABINET

The Prime Minister attracts extensive media attention. Much is written about the person in the office. During her occupancy of No. 10 Downing Street, Margaret Thatcher attracted particular attention. She was the first Prime Minister to generate an 'ism' (Thatcherism). When she left office, she was Britain's longest continuously serving Prime Minister (eleven years and six months) since Lord Liverpool at the beginning of the 19th Century. Much has been written about her,[14] and doubtless will continue to be written about her, both by admirers and detractors. The focus will tend to be the individual, as will the works about her successor, John Major. What remains remarkable is the dearth of detached and scholarly

analyses of relations between Prime Minister and Cabinet, both generally and specifically for the period from 1979 to 1990.

Though Prime Ministers are variously studied, hardly any works have
appeared on the premiership as such, analysing its position in the context
of the wider political system. The principal work of contemporary
relevance is a reader, Anthony King's *The British Prime Minister*, first
published in 1969 but appearing in revised form in 1985. The past twenty
years have been remarkable for the absence of a good, substantial, single-
author analysis.

The Cabinet has fared a little better. There are a number, though still
few, works on the subject, ranging from John Mackintosh's classic *The
British Cabinet,* first published in 1962, to the more recent study, *Cabinet*
(1986) by Peter Hennessy.[15] They have been supplemented by memoirs
and, since the 1970s, by the publication of diaries by a number of those
who have sat at the Cabinet table.[16] What we know about PM–Cabinet
relations is drawn largely from these disparate and – in the case of
memoirs and diaries – not always dispassionate sources.

Various writers have argued that a form of Prime Ministerial government has developed, displacing that form of government – Cabinet
government – which is assumed to have characterised British government for more than a century. Richard Crossman initiated the debate in
the 1960s;[17] it was renewed in the 1970s by Tony Benn and Brian
Sedgemore[18] and took on a new prominence in the 1980s during the
premiership of Margaret Thatcher. The Thatcher premiership is generally offered as the epitome of Prime Ministerial Government. Yet such
a characterisation derives principally from anecdote, memoirs from
interested parties and casual observation, especially of Margaret Thatcher's style of leadership. It was often reinforced during the 1980s by
popular satire. In a sketch in the *Spitting Image* television series, Margaret
Thatcher was shown seated at a dinner table with the members of her
Cabinet. After ordering meat, she was asked: 'What about the vegetables?'
'Oh', she replied, 'they'll have the same!' It was a skit that reinforced the
image that friend and foe alike of Mrs Thatcher appeared keen to convey;
Mrs Thatcher herself was reputed to enjoy the observation that she was
'the only man in the Cabinet'.

But what truth is there in the popular perception? Have recent Prime
Ministers, Margaret Thatcher in particular, dominated the Cabinet to
such an extent that it is possible to assert that the country is governed by
the Prime Minister? (And it is important to remember that the debate

takes place largely within the context of the relationship of Prime Minister to Cabinet.[19]) And, if so, is the trend an irreversible one?

In *Cabinet*, Peter Hennessy in one chapter addressed the position of the Cabinet in the period between 1979 and 1986 and in another considered 'the Quality of Cabinet Government'.[20] In the years following the book's publication, he turned his attention to the civil service, the fruits of his labours appearing in his tome *Whitehall* in 1989.[21] In his chapter in this volume, he returns to the question of PM–Cabinet relations.

Reviewing the Thatcher premiership, his conclusion about the death of Cabinet government is not dissimilar to Mark Twain's response to the announcement of his own death. It is greatly exaggerated. As Hennessy records, 'the colours are not that primary, not quite that stark'. Critics have tended to confuse style with substance. Despite the techniques employed by Margaret Thatcher – and, as Hennessy records, they were substantial – the key function of Cabinet government remained operational. Cabinet government under the Thatcher premiership was 'peeky but not poorly'. It is a conclusion with profound implications for the thesis of Prime Ministerial government. If Cabinet government survived, albeit with difficulty, during the era of the most powerful of recent premiers, then it has an existence and a future neither imagined or conceded by those who seek to put an end to what Tony Benn called an 'Absolute Premiership'.

THE JUDICIARY

Judicial independence is a vital constituent of the British constitution. The legal system stands separate from the partisan arena of policy making. The Queen-in-Parliament makes the law. The courts then interpret and apply that law, impartially and free from outside interference.

The independence of the legal system, declared Lord Scarman in his 1974 Hamlyn Lecture, is 'a bulwark against oppression and tyranny, no matter who be the potential oppressor or tyrant'.[22] Various barriers have been erected, by statute or convention, to protect the courts from the influence of government and Parliament. Since the Act of Settlement, senior judges have held office 'during good behaviour' and can be removed only by the Queen following an address by both Houses of Parliament.[23] Judicial salaries are a charge upon the Consolidated Fund, thus avoiding being voted annually by Parliament. By its own resolution, the House of Commons prohibits references to matters that are under adjudication by the courts (*sub judice*). By convention, the same self-censorship is observed by ministers and civil servants.

This independence is jealousy guarded by judges and, indeed, by the legal profession generally. The independence of the courts, it is argued, entails protecting the independence of those who are its officers. 'Under our system of law', declared Lord Hailsham, 'the judiciary is recruited solely from successful practitioners of the law. The independence of the judiciary depends more upon the independence and integrity of the legal profession than upon any other single factor.'[24] Judges and lawyers are thus wary of any threat to the independence of the system that they essentially created and sustain.[25]

Threats to this independence have traditionally been perceived as coming from critics on the left who view with suspicion a judiciary that is largely conservative in disposition and – not unrelated – white, male and upper-middle-class in background. The most recent and potent expression of this viewpoint has come from J. A. G. Griffith in *The Politics of the Judiciary,* first published in 1977. As a result of their education and training, he argues, judges share a homogeneous set of values which, to them, represent the public interest. That public interest is generally construed to favour law and order, property rights and the interests of the state at times of perceived threat.[26] The answer, according to such critics, is reform of the judiciary, with judges drawn from more socially representative backgrounds, and with legislation, rather than judicial discretion, being relied on to define and protect individual and minority rights.

More recently, however, there have been fears of a challenge from the right. In part, this stems from the government's use of legislation to reverse the outcome of cases which have gone against it. This, though, entails the use of existing powers under the constitution. What has particularly alarmed judges and barristers alike has been the more recent proposals of government to reform the legal profession. At the beginning of 1989 the Lord Chancellor's Department published three Green Papers proposing major changes in the organisation of the profession. They constituted part of an attempt by government to make the legal system more efficient – and cost-effective – as a public service. Among the government's Green Paper proposals were the removal of the monopoly enjoyed by barristers to plead cases before superior courts and for those who enjoyed rights of audience to obtain certificates of advocacy and to be subject to a code of conduct. The Lord Chancellor, advised by his

Advisory Committee on Legal Education and Conduct, was to be responsible for the recognition of the professional bodies that would grant the certificates and would determine the code of conduct. 'The Government', declared one of the Green Papers, 'is not prepared to leave it to the legal profession to settle the principles which these codes should adopt.'

The legal profession immediately hoisted its battle standard. It deployed its members in the House of Lords. When the Green Papers were debated in the House on a Friday, more than fifty peers had put their names down to take part in the debate. Instead of rising after two or three hours, the House sat for more than twelve hours, from 9.30 a.m. until 10.41 p.m. During this unprecedented sitting, the government's proposals were subject to a barrage of criticism; it was clear that had Lord Hailsham still been on the Woolsack they would never have seen the light of day. The stance taken by the judges was put clearly by the Lord Chief Justice, Lord Lane:

> In some common law jurisdictions in other parts of the world, with British-style systems of government, the administration of justice has indeed come under the heel of government. Judges there are no longer independent. The principle of the rule of law is observed so long as it suits the government and no longer. The private legal profession is bullied. We are told, and people say, 'Of course, it couldn't happen here'. Could it not? The growth in the powers of the executive, and therefore of the government, over the administration of justice has steadily increased in recent years. The signs are that it will extend still further, and one asks whether we are now seeing tools being fashioned which by some future, perhaps less scrupulous government may be used to weaken the independent administration of justice and so undermine the rule of law.[27]

To what extent, then, is the independence of the judiciary under threat? It is this question that Gavin Drewry addresses in Chapter 3. He draws together the components of the perceived threat – extending beyond the Green Paper proposals and the general thrust of government policy aimed at achieving a more efficient public service to encompass also the proposal variously made for a Department of Justice – and argues cogently that, if anything, there is as much a threat to judicial independence in the judges' response to these developments as in the developments themselves. Achieving greater efficiency in service is not incompatible with maintaining the principle of judicial neutrality. Judicial independence is not an end in itself but a means to an end. It is a prerequisite for neutrality. Yet both independence and neutrality rest on a subjective as well as an objective base: the courts have to be seen to be both independent and neutral. 'Public perceptions of the judiciary, and confidence in the judicial process itself', writes Drewry, 'must surely be influenced for the worse by their exclusiveness, their defensiveness, their complacency and their propensity to attack their critics with stridently expressed constitutional platitudes in lieu of reasoned argument – the Green Paper debates are a case in point.' The problem, he suggests, is exacerbated by lack of parliamentary accountability and by the secrecy surrounding matters pertaining to judicial appointments.

By resisting change, especially any change that threatens their conduct of business, training and means of appointment (either substantively or through opening it up to parliamentary scrutiny), on the grounds that it constitutes a threat to judicial independence, the judges may thus constitute a substantial threat to that which they seek to defend. It is an important and stimulating argument. It provides a valuable corrective to the dominant – and very influential – view espoused by judges and the Bar.

PARLIAMENT

Parliament generally gets a bad press: journalists, academics and civil servants are prone to dismiss it as a peripheral, and increasingly irrelevant, body in the British polity. It is condemned as constituting neither a policy-making body nor one that can constrain a power-accreting government. 'The notion of Parliament as the sole guardian of liberty', declared Geoffrey Robertson, 'is risible';[28] there may be occasional backbench revolts, 'but most MPs will cower under the three-line whip'.[29] And the position is seen as having worsened under the Thatcher administration. The government, according to Andrew Gamble, has done very little to reverse the decline of Parliament: 'The failure to make Parliament more representative and more central to political debate made the executive more like an elective dictatorship than ever.'[30]

Parliament thus stands condemned as little more than a cosmetic part of the constitutional framework. 'A bill before the House signals the end of the real battle and the start of a squabble over detail. It is the tiresome but essential task of window-dressing.'[31] This view appears pervasive among the literature promoting reform of the Constitution. Parliament is either dismissed in a relatively short space or not mentioned at all. But how justified is this dismissive view?

The criticisms of Parliament suffer from two basic defects. One is that there is no clear delineation of what Parliament is actually expected to do. The second is that, in arguing that it is not doing it as well as it used to, no evidence is presented to demonstrate that Parliament was actually, doing the job better at some previous time. In other words, 'decline' is asserted but never proved.

Parliament is a multi-functional body having consequences for the political system other than those on which critics principally focus.[32] Even within the domain of policy-making – on which critics concentrate – it is not quite the irrelevant body that it is made out to be. I have elsewhere drawn attention to the change in parliamentary behaviour that has taken place since 1970. Members of Parliament – and peers – are no longer the lobby fodder they once were.[33] In my chapter for this volume I look at a more recent – and little surveyed – development: the growth of parliamentary lobbying. Over the past few years, pressure groups have in effect 'discovered' Parliament. But it is not just groups: constituents are more active than ever before in making demands of MPs.

What are the causes and implications of this development? Literature on the subject is relatively sparse: some books from political consultants (lobbyists) explaining how to lobby, and a substantial academic tome, *Parliament and Pressure Politics*,[34] analysing lobbying by organised groups, constitute the principal material. In my chapter I have attempted to provide a synoptic overview and to assess the implications for Parliament as a policy-influencing legislature.

The basic import of the chapter is that Parliament is essentially a more open institution. The protective shield erected by party – creating a 'closed' institution – has been, if not worn away, at least rusted at the edges. Groups and constituents are able to achieve a greater input, that input providing parliamentarians with information and advice that can now be pitted against that offered by government. The consequence is more critical scrutiny of government than that which was possible before.

Party remains the essential point of reference for MPs and peers; necessarily so.[35] There is little chance of the UK emulating the experience of the United States. We have a policy-influencing, not a policy-making, legislature: within that context, there is certainly much more that could be done to strengthen it.[36] But Parliament is not the irrelevant, and increasingly irrelevant, 'window dressing' body that critics make it out to be.

LOCAL GOVERNMENT

Twenty years ago, Howard Elcock has recorded, local government was a 'yawn' subject. 'Now', he writes, 'there is a stimulating, varied and provocative literature being written.... Diversity and perhaps most of all excitement, have been born of adversity.'[37] It is a view echoed by Rod Rhodes in his contribution to this volume. Local government is very much on the agenda of political debate; it is a subject of extensive academic interest.

Much of the literature focuses on the adversity referred to by Elcock. Fiscal constraints, legislation and administrative action have been employed by government to alter radically the sub-national government of the country. In the first two Parliaments of the Conservative administration (1979–87), more than forty bills were introduced that affected local government in one way or another; by 1990 the figure had reached fifty. For many critics the measures were the product of a government intent on centralising power in its own hands. 'Britain', declared Paul Hirst, 'is a highly centralised state and it has become more centralised during the Conservatives' ten years in office. ... The autonomy of local government has been relentlessly diminished by Conservative legislation and administrative action.'[38]

This power-centralisation thesis is now well established in the literature; it constitutes the most notable theme.[39] A number of other interpretations have been offered. These include the party-advantage thesis – changes being wrought (abolition of the GLC and the metropolitan counties, introduction of the community charge) that will disadvantage the Labour Party – and the public-choice thesis, the imperatives of the market being applied to local authorities.[40] We thus have different explanations of the stance taken by central government towards local government over the past decade. How persuasive are they?

Rod Rhodes addresses the question by assessing the actual effects of government policy and by looking at the trends in government policy on a Parliament-by-Parliament basis. The government's relations with local government, he argues, have been marked more by unintended consequences than by an intended 'revolution' in local government. The distinctive trend that many seek to identify is not there. Local government restraint is not peculiar to the Thatcher administration. And centralisation is not the defining and exclusive characteristic of government policy toward local government. There has, Rhodes concedes, been some centralisation, but there is also clear evidence of de-centralisation.

What, then, is the clear, defining characteristic of government policy since 1979? The answer effectively is that there has not been one. Government policy has shifted from Parliament to Parliament, the most significant consequence of which has not been effective centralisation of power but rather what Rhodes terms a 'policy mess'. Neither level of government, he contends, is now in a position to achieve its policy objectives.

Central government, then, has not brought about a revolution and the future direction of local government is far from clear. Rhodes sketches four directions in which local government may go: centralisation, the contract authority, community government and differentiation. Whatever happens, the outcome is likely to be unpredictable. Too many complexities exist to offer a mono-causal explanation of developments in centre–local government relations over the past decade; and those complexities prevent the future being predicted with any degree of confidence. Rhodes's chapter stands as a valuable challenge to those who embark on such an exercise.

THE EUROPEAN COMMUNITY

Britain's relations with the European Community have never been anything less than ambiguous. Membership of the Community was a contentious issue in the 1960s and early 1970s. Both the Conservative and Labour parties were badly divided and the Heath Government in 1972 managed to achieve the Second Reading of the European Communities Bill only after making the vote one of confidence: even then, 15 government backbenchers voted against it.[41] It has remained a contentious issue since the UK became a member on 1 January 1973. It came to the fore in political debate in 1975 when the first UK-wide referendum was held to determine whether the country should remain a member on the terms renegotiated by the Labour government;[42] and it has generally been an issue since 1979 and more especially since Mrs Thatcher's speech at the College of Europe in Bruges in September 1988. It was disagreement with the Prime Minister's approach to the Community that prompted a Conservative backbencher, Sir Anthony Meyer, to challenge Mrs Thatcher for the Conservative Party leadership in December 1989.[43] It was the catalyst for the events that led to her resignation the following year.

For much of the first decade of membership the debate revolved around whether Britain should remain a member of the Community. Though the referendum produced a large majority for remaining a member (17.4 million in favour versus 8.5 million against) the issue was not quite stilled.[44] In the second decade of membership the debate revolved around what form the Community would take. Two predominant and opposing views emerged. On the one side were the integrationists, those favouring a more integrated Community including economic and monetary union. On the other side were the functionalists, those who saw the Community as a collection of sovereign nation-states agreeing on measures to achieve a single market in goods, capital and labour. The President of the Commission of the EC, Jacques Delors, emerged as the most forceful proponent of the former school. Mrs Thatcher championed the latter view. For integrationists, achieving a single market was but part of an overall package. For functionalists it was an end in itself.

The debate reached a new plane following Mrs Thatcher's Bruges speech. 'To try to suppress nationhood and concentrate power at the centre of a European conglomerate', she declared, 'would jeopardise the objectives we seek to achieve.' It was a development she would not countenance. 'We have not successfully rolled back the frontiers of the state in Britain only to see them reimposed at a European level.'[45] For M. Delors – who produced the Delors Report outlining a three-stage process towards economic and monetary union – the steps already taken constituted part of an 'irretrievable process'.[46]

Developments in Eastern Europe in 1989 and 1990 added considerably to the debate. With the collapse of the demarcation between East and West should the emphasis remain on moving forward rapidly to achieve integration of the existing Community (deepening the Community) or should emphasis shift to trying to encompass the states of Eastern Europe (widening the Community)? For Mrs Thatcher widening the Community took precedence. Speaking in Aspen, Colorado, in August 1990 she declared that the peoples of Eastern Europe 'had not thrown off central command and control in their own countries only to find them reincarnated in the European Community. ... We must find a structure for the Community which accommodates their diversity and preserves their tradition, their institutions, their nationhood.'[47] For M. Delors, deepening takes precedence. Other integrationists have argued that there is not necessarily a conflict between deepening and widening.[48]

Given that there is no one view that has made the running in recent debate, the issue of the EC requires somewhat different treatment.

Consequently two contributions have been invited, analysing the present position from conflicting perspectives. Stanley Clinton-Davis – now Lord Clinton-Davis – served as a member of the Commission of the EC from 1985 to 1989. Enoch Powell is a long-standing opponent of British membership of the Community: he voted consistently against the European Communities Bill in 1972 – including on Second Reading – and was one of only six Conservative Members of Parliament in 1950 to abstain from supporting a motion moved by Anthony Eden requesting the Attlee Government to accept the invitation to take part in the discussions on the Schuman Plan.[49]

For Lord Clinton-Davis Britain has not gone as far as it should as a member of the EC; for Enoch Powell it has gone too far. The Single European Act, argues Lord Clinton-Davis, constitutes more than a framework for achieving a single market; 'it is the design for the construction of a true community'. There is the danger, he contends, of Britain being left behind when the important decisions on monetary union are taken. 'Here, as in other areas, the 1990s may see Europe advancing at two speeds with Britain holding back in the slow lane. The risk to Britain as a financial centre are all too clear.' Rather than a widening of the Community, he foresees an association with the members of EFTA (the European Free Trade Area) and the countries of Eastern Europe. Within the Community he sees the need to strengthen and to democratise its institutions. How far and how fast the tools provided by the Single European Act are used to draw the Community together depends on men and women of vision and the young people who will be the first true Europeans. 'They will be helped by increased opportunities for exchanges, visits and learning languages. But for us in Britain, so much needs to change.'

Enoch Powell would like to see events moving in a direction completely different to that of an integrated Community. The forces that propelled the United Kingdom into a reluctant membership are, he believes, dissolving. He contends that Europe is now 'reverting to type'. As a result of the events in Eastern Europe the nation-state is being rediscovered and American interest and involvement in Western Europe waning. He thus foresees a situation in which the people of the United Kingdom, or more particularly England, may bestir themselves to regain the 'eternal jewel' of parliamentary sovereignty. He does not predict that this will happen, but he looks ahead with some hopefulness to what he considers a Promised Land that will be denied him.

Both contributions, from totally different perspectives, provide important and provocative challenges to much present thinking about the European Community. Should the British government be more positive in its approach to the Community, embracing the concept of a community that extends beyond a single market? Or should it be more radical in moving in the opposite direction, to the point where it acts to strengthen parliamentary sovereignty? It is difficult for the reader to adopt a neutral stance in the face of two challenging chapters.

REFORM OF THE CONSTITUTION

The contributions to this volume that address particular aspects of contemporary debate challenge many of the views now prevalent in that debate. The concluding chapter is no exception. It addresses the case now being advanced for a reformulation of the Constitution – for a new constitutional settlement, to use the language of Lord Scarman – and one which has been making most of the running in debate. Few if any significant responses have been penned. Chapter 8 seeks to fill this important gap by offering a response to the case for change.

The pressure for a new constitutional settlement has, as we have seen, grown in recent years. Charter '88 stands essentially as the rallying banner for the reformers. In Chapter 8 I sketch the background to the growth of the pressure for reform and detail the case advanced for a new constitutional settlement. I then provide my riposte to that case. The argument advanced by Charter '88 is, I contend, based on a false premiss, distorted in perception and inadequate as a remedy for the ills it claims to exist in the constitutional framework. And by building up expectations it cannot hope to meet, as well as by distracting attention from other important issues (including constitutional issues), it is dangerous to the health of the body politic.

If there is to be constitutional reform it should be the consequence of considered debate; likewise if reform is to be rejected it should be the consequence of reasoned deliberation rather than of *force majeure* or simple inertia. I am opposed to radical constitutional surgery and I am happy to contribute to the debate by explaining why.

NOTES

1. There is no one agreed definition. The one given here is the one I consider to be most useful and have used consistently in my other writings. It is drawn from O. Hood Phillips, *Constitutional and Administrative Law*, 6th edn (London: Sweet & Maxwell, 1978) p. 5.
2. N. Johnson, *In Search of the Constitution* (London: Methuen, 1980) pp. 31–2.
3. G. Sartori, *Parties and the Party System: A Framework for Analysis* (Cambridge: Cambridge University Press, 1976) p. 185.
4. A. Lester, 'The Constitution: Decline and Renewal', in J. Jowell and D. Oliver (eds), *The Changing Constitution* (Oxford: Oxford University Press, 1985) p. 273.
5. A. Wright, 'British Socialists and the British Constitution', *Parliamentary Affairs*, 43 (3), July 1990, p. 325.
6. A. Lester, *Democracy and Individual Rights* (London: Fabian Society, 1968); J. MacDonald, *A Bill of Rights* (London: Liberal Party, 1969); Q. Hogg, *New Charter* (London: Conservative Political Centre, 1969); 0. Hood Phillips, *Reform of the Constitution* (London: Chatto & Windus/Charles Knight, 1970).
7. Sir L. Scarman, *English Law – The New Dimension* (London: Stevens, 1974); Lord Hailsham, *Elective Dictatorship* (London: British Broadcasting Corporation, 1976).
8. Scarman, *English Law*, p. 74.
9. See P. Norton, *The Constitution in Flux* (Oxford: Martin Robertson, 1982), chs 9, 12 and 13, and also the conclusion to this volume.
10. See P. Norton and J. Hayward, 'Retrospective Reflections', in J. Hayward and P. Norton (eds), *The Political Science of British Politics* (Brighton: Wheatsheaf, 1986) pp . 205–6.
11. See J. Dearlove, 'Bringing the Constitution Back In: Political Science and the State', *Political Studies*, 37 (4), December 1989, pp. 521–39; and D. Oliver, 'The Literature on the Constitution', *Contemporary Record*, 3 (1), Autumn 1989, pp. 44–5.
12. 'A Modern Democracy', in *Meet the Challenge, Make the Change* (London: Labour Party, 1989) pp. 55–8.
13. On political science, see Dearlove, 'Bringing the Constitution Back In'.
14. The literature on Mrs Thatcher, Thatcherism and the Thatcher government is voluminous. To take but the principal works published in the period from 1987 we have: K. Minogue and M. Biddiss (eds), *Thatcherism: Personality and Politics* (London: Macmillan, 1987); D. Kavanagh, *Thatcherism and British Politics* (Oxford: Oxford University Press, 1987, 2nd edn, 1990); P. Jenkins, *Mrs Thatcher's Revolution* (London: Jonathan Cape, 1987); G. Owen (ed.), *The Thatcher Years* (London: Financial Times, 1987); A. Gamble, *The Free Economy and the Strong State* (London: Macmillan, 1988); R. Skidelsky (ed.), *Thatcherism* (Oxford: Blackwell, 1988); B. Jessop *et al.*, *Thatcherism: A Tale of Two Nations* (Cambridge: Polity Press, 1988); S. Hall, *The Hard Road to Renewal* (London: Verso, 1988); H. Young, *One of Us* (London: Macmillan, 1989); P. Riddell, *The Thatcher Decade* (Oxford: Blackwell, 1989); D. Kavanagh and A. Seldon (eds), *The Thatcher Effect* (Oxford: Oxford University Press, 1989); P. Hirst, *After Thatcher* (London: Collins, 1989) and S. P. Savage and L. Robins (eds), *Public Policy Under Thatcher* (London: Macmillan, 1990). The list is not exhaustive.
15. Other works on the Cabinet include P. Gordon Walker, *The Cabinet*, rev. edn (London: Fontana, 1972); M. Rush, *The Cabinet and Policy Formation* (London: Longman, 1984); and – in comparative perspective – T. T. Mackie and B. Hogwood (eds), *Unlocking the Cabinet* (London: Sage, 1985).
16. R. H. S. Crossman, *The Diaries of a Cabinet Minister*, 3 vols (London: Hamish Hamilton/Jonathan Cape, 1975, 1976, 1977); B. Castle, *The Castle Diaries, 1974–*

76 (London: Weidenfeld & Nicolson, 1980); T. Benn, *Out of the Wilderness: Diaries, 1963–67* (London: Hutchinson, 1987), and *Office Without Power: Diaries, 1968–72* (London: Hutchinson, 1988).

17. R. H. S. Crossman, Introduction to W. Bagehot, *The English Constitution* (first published 1867; London: Fontana, 1963). See also G. W. Jones, 'The Prime Minister's Powers', *Parliamentary Affairs*, 18, 1965, pp. 167–85; and A. H. Brown, 'Prime Ministerial Power (Part II)', *Public Law*, Summer 1968, pp. 96–118.

18. T. Benn, 'The Case for a Constitutional Premiership', *Parliamentary Affairs*, 33 (1), Winter 1980, pp. 7–33; and B. Sedgemore, *The Secret Constitution* (London: Hodder & Stoughton, 1980).

19. See P. Norton, 'Prime Ministerial Power', *Social Studies Review*, 3 (3), January 1988, pp. 108–15.

20. P. Hennessy, *Cabinet* (Oxford: Blackwell, 1986), chs 3 and 5.

21. P. Hennessy, *Whitehall* (London: Secker & Warburg, 1989).

22. Scarman, *English Law*, p. 6.

23. Only John Barrington, an Irish judge, has suffered this fate: he was removed in 1830 after it was found he had misappropriated litigants' money and had ceased to perform his judicial duties.

24. *House of Lords Debates*, vol. 505, c. 1333.

25. The importance of the legal system as the creation of the judges is variously stressed by jurists: see especially Scarman, *English Law*, p. 6.

26 J. A. G. Griffith, *The Politics of the Judiciary* (London: Fontana, 1977) p. 195.

27 *House of Lords Debates*, vol. 505, c. 1331.

28. G. Robertson, *Freedom, the Individual and the Law*, 6th edn (London: Penguin, 1989) p. 400.

29. Ibid., p. 388.

30. A. Gamble, 'The Thatcher Decade in Perspective', in P. Dunleavy, A. Gamble and G. Peele (eds), *Developments in British Politics 3* (London: Macmillan, 1990) p. 345.

31. K. D. Ewing and C. A. Gearty, *Freedom Under Thatcher: Civil Liberties in Modern Britain* (Oxford: Oxford University Press, 1990) p. 6.

32. See P. Norton, 'Parliament in the United Kingdom: Balancing Effectiveness and Consent?', *West European Politics*, 13 (3), July 1990, pp. 10–31.

33. P. Norton, *Dissension in the House of Commons, 1945–74* (London: Macmillan, 1975), *Conservative Dissidents* (London: Temple Smith, 1978), *Dissension in the House of Commons, 1974–1979* (Oxford: Oxford University Press, 1980), 'The House of Commons: Behavioural Changes', in P. Norton (ed.), *Parliament in the 1980s* (Oxford: Blackwell, 1985) pp. 22–47.

34. M. Rush (ed.), *Parliament and Pressure Politics* (Oxford: Oxford University Press, 1990). See also C. Grantham, 'Parliament and Political Consultants', *Parliamentary Affairs*, 42 (4), October 1989, pp. 503–18.

35. For a justification for 'necessarily so', see P. Norton, 'The Norton View', in D. Judge (ed.), *The Politics of Parliamentary Reform* (London: Heinemann, 1983) pp. 54–69; and P. Riddell, 'In Defence of Parliament', *Contemporary Record*, 3 (1), Autumn 1989, pp. 6–9.

36. On the distinction between policy-making and policy-influencing, see P. Norton, 'Parliament and Policy in Britain: the House of Commons as a Policy Influencer', *Teaching Politics*, 13 (2), May 1984, pp. 198–221. On what might be done to strengthen the institution, see for example P. Norton, 'Memorandum of Evidence', *House of Commons Select Committee on Procedure: The Working of the Select Committee System*, Session 1989/90, Minutes of Evidence: 14 February 1990, HC 19–viii, pp. 139–46.

37. H. Elcock, 'What Values for Urban Politics?', *Parliamentary Affairs*, 43 (3), July 1990, pp. 387–8.
38. P. Hirst, *After Thatcher* (London: Collins, 1989) p. 44.
39. See, for example, M. Goldsmith and K. Newton, 'Central–Local Government Relations: the Irresistible Rise of Centralised Power', *West European Politics*, 6, 1983, pp. 216–33; G. W. Jones and J. Stewart, *The Case for Local Government* (London: George Allen & Unwin, 1985), M. Loughlin, *Local Government in the Modern State* (London: Sweet & Maxwell, 1986); and M. Parkinson (ed.), *Reshaping Local Government* (London: Policy Journals, 1987).
40. These are well summarised in G. Stoker, 'Government Beyond Whitehall ', in Dunleavy *et al.* (eds), *Developments in British Politics 3*, pp. 140–7.
41. *House of Commons Debates*, vol. 831, c 753–8. See also Norton, *Conservative Dissidents*, pp. 64–82.
42. See A. King, *Britain Says Yes* (Washington, D.C.: American Enterprise Institute, 1977).
43. See P. Norton, 'Mrs Thatcher and the Parliamentary Conservative Party, 1989–1990', *Parliamentary Affairs*, 43 (3). July 1990, pp. 252–4.
44. See Norton, *The Constitution in Flux*, ch. 8.
45. M. Thatcher, *Britain and Europe* (London: Conservative Political Centre, 1988) p. 4.
46. House of Commons Library, *Brussels, Westminster and the Single European Act*, Background Paper no. 220 (London: House of Commons Library, 1988) pp. 21–2.
47. *The Economist*, 11 August 1990, p. 14
48. See ibid.
49. *House of Commons Debates*, vol. 476, c. 2175–82. See also A. Roth, *Enoch Powell: Tory Tribune* (London: Macdonald, 1970) pp. 67–8.

2. How Much Room at the Top? Margaret Thatcher, the Cabinet and Power-Sharing

Peter Hennessy

I have a predisposition when considering Cabinet government to tilt in favour of shared, collective discussion as a prelude to decision-taking. Short cuts, whether taken in the name of efficiency or confidentiality, make me nervous. It is a prejudice I share with my journalistic hero, Walter Bagehot. Bagehot dilated on this crucial ingredient of top policy-making in a democracy not in his celebrated book *The English Constitution*[1] but in a less-known work written as a series of essays in the *Fortnightly Review* in the late 1860s and published in 1872 with the odd title *Physics and Politics* and the even odder sub-title: 'Thoughts on the Application of the Principles of "Natural Selection" and "Inheritance" to Political Society'.[2]

In it Bagehot argued the case that discussion is the key chemical in a modern political system, both dissolving ancient custom and superstition and acting as a catalyst to new thought and innovation. 'The mere putting up of a subject to discussion, with the object of being guided by that discussion, is a clear admission that that subject is in no degree settled by established rule, and that men are free to choose in it', was how he put it.[3]

Part of the enduring brilliance of Bagehot (whose portrait, incidentally, hangs above my desk in Walthamstow as an aid to inspiration)[4] is not just the relevance of his thinking to current preoccupations but his extraordinary ability to foreshadow the insights of generations several decades unborn at the time he wrote. Consider this passage from *Physics and Politics* not merely for the truth of what it says about discussion as an aid to tolerance, but also as a pre-echo of J. K. Galbraith's famous theory of the 'conventional wisdom' expressed in his *The Affluent Society* in 1958.[5] 'Tolerance' wrote Bagehot in 1872:

is learned in discussion, and, as history shows is only so learned. In all customary societies bigotry is the ruling principle. In rude places to this day anyone who says anything new is looked on with suspicion and is persecuted by opinion if not injured by penalty. One of the greatest pains to human nature is the pain of a new idea. It is, as common people say so 'upsetting'; it makes you think that, after all, your favourite notions may be wrong, your firmest beliefs ill founded; it is certain that till now there was no place allotted in your mind to the new and startling inhabitant, and now that it has conquered an entrance, you do not at once see which of your old ideas it will or will not turn out, with which of them it can be reconciled, and with which it is at essential enmity. Naturally, therefore, common men hate a new idea, and are disposed more or less to ill-treat the original man who brings it.

Even nations with long habits of discussion are intolerant enough. In England where there is on the whole probably a freer discussion of a greater number of subjects than ever was before in the world, we know how much power bigotry retains. But discussion, to be successful, requires tolerance.[6]

Here is the kernel of the matter of Margaret Thatcher and the pursuit of Cabinet government in the British tradition: was it compatible with conviction politics, with her assertion three months before taking office in a celebrated interview with Kenneth Harris that 'It must be a conviction government. As Prime Minister I could not waste time having any internal arguments'?[7] This was no throw-away line. It was sandwiched between two long disquisitions on the only way to proceed as she saw it. They are rarely referred to, unlike that pair of sentences which flash regularly in neon in the recall of political commentators. But they are worth pondering because Mrs Thatcher, in another characteristic that makes her unique among recent occupants of No. 10, had a habit of telling everyone in advance precisely what she intended to do before striding off to do it. On this occasion she began by telling Kenneth Harris:

If you're going to do the things you want to do – and I'm only in politics to do things – you've got to have a togetherness and unity in your Cabinet. There are two ways of making a Cabinet. One way is to have in it people who represent all the different view points within the party, within the broad philosophy. The other way is to have in it only the people who want to go in the direction in which every instinct tells me we have to go. Clearly, steadily, firmly, with resolution. We've got to go in an agreed and clear direction.[8]

Now came the famous line about a 'conviction Cabinet'. She went on: 'It's the same with the Shadow Cabinet. We've got to be together as a team.'

At this point she succumbed to Harold Wilson's disease of reducing matters of state to the level of a football pitch: 'A football manager wouldn't put anyone, however brilliant, in his team if he believed that player couldn't work together with the rest.'

This, incidentally, is the reason Neville Chamberlain gave Leslie Hore-Belisha for keeping Churchill out of his prewar Cabinet.[9] Roy Jenkins has a point when he says that of all other twentieth-century premiers, Mrs Thatcher is most like Chamberlain in her 'force of will combined with intolerance, and combined with this ability to see a number of limited things'.[10]

Back to Mrs Thatcher talking to Ken Harris in February 1979:

> I've got to have togetherness. There must be a dedication to a purpose, agreement about direction. As leader I have a duty to try and inspire that. If you choose a team in which you encounter a basic disagreement, you will not be able to carry out a programme, you won't be able to govern. I think that's probably what is wrong with the present Labour Cabinet; there are two basic parties in it, two basic philosophies. We, on the other hand, have a Shadow Cabinet with a unity of purpose. When the time comes to form a real Cabinet with equal unity of purpose and a sense of dedication to it, it must be a Cabinet that works on something much more than pragmatism or consensus. It must be a *conviction* Cabinet.[11]

There. We were well and truly warned. And indeed a formidable case can be made out to suggest that what we read in our *Observers* on that February Sunday in 1979 is precisely what we got. It's partly because Margaret Thatcher's oft-declared claim to have 'changed everything' was taken far too facilely at its face value. And partly it's to do with the great pile of evidence which has accumulated from the statements of those who were expunged from the Cabinet room, for one reason or another, during the Thatcher premiership.

When you examine them, line by line, it's easy to see how the view of an over-mighty premiership – of a Prime Minister moving us away from a Cabinet system of government, based on the cardinal principle of collective decision-taking and responsibility, to a presidential one built around a single figure of commanding power and overriding purpose – almost gained the status of 'conventional wisdom' and therefore of a self-evident truth of the 'it stands to reason' variety.

Let me pull out a few gems from my bag of ready quotations. First, Norman St John-Stevas (or Lord St John of Fawsley as we must now get used to calling him), one of the first to go for among other things the unusual offence of causing laughter with his asides about 'the Blessed Margaret' and the 'Leaderene'.[12] 'There is no doubt that as regards the

Cabinet', he wrote in 1986, 'the most commanding Prime Minister of modern times has been the present incumbent, Mrs Thatcher. Convinced of both her own rectitude and ability she has tended to reduce the Cabinet to subservience.'[13]

Next Lord Soames, removed for refusing to be the hammer of the civil service and a huge, somewhat irascible roly-poly of a man who had worked, in one way or another, with every postwar Conservative premier. 'She was not really running a team', he told me from his sickbed in the spring of 1984, clothed in a great marquee of a silken dressing gown. 'Every time you have a Prime Minister who wants to take all the decisions, it mainly leads to bad results. Attlee didn't. That's why he was so damn good. Macmillan didn't. The nearest parallel to Maggie is Ted.'[14]

The Westland Affair in the opening days of 1986 brought Sir Ian Gilmour (sacked liked Soames in 1981, in this case to his evident relief) on to the television screen to inform the public that being a good listener was not one of Mrs Thatcher's virtues[15] and to claim that there had been 'a downgrading of Cabinet government'.[16] The funniest contribution on this theme came just before the Westland crisis from the minister still in the Cabinet, Peter Walker, who delighted in expressing his view as a merry quip at after-lunch speeches. He would quote the Duke of Wellington's reaction to his first Cabinet meeting as Prime Minister: 'An extraordinary affair. I gave them their orders and they wanted to stay and discuss them.' Then he would pause and say: 'I'm so glad we don't have Prime Ministers like that today.'[17]

Perhaps the most graphic depiction of life behind the green baize door in No. 10 to come from a deposed minister occurred in a radio interview between David Howell and myself in 1985. 'If by "conviction government" ', he told me:

> it is meant that certain slogans were going to be elevated and written in tablets of stone and used as the putdown at the end of every argument, then, of course, that is indeed what happened. ... Of course there is a deterring effect if one knows that one's going to go not into a discussion where various points of view will be weighed and gradually a view may be achieved, but into a huge argument where tremendous battle lines will be drawn up and everyone who doesn't fall into line will be hit on the head.[18]

Now the impression of what Harold Macmillan called 'a brilliant tyrant surrounded by mediocrities'[19] in her Cabinet room spread so far and so thoroughly abroad that by the time the 1983 Parliament was dissolved the lady and her style became an issue in their own right at the 1987 General Election, the first time this had happened since 1922 when Bonar Law made much of Lloyd George's alleged assault on the Constitution through the creation of such wildly revolutionary institutions as the Cabinet Office.

David Steel began the attack, on what was widely seen as by now a thoroughly over-mighty premiership, two days before the election was called, accusing the Prime Minister of 'having virtually abolished Cabinet government and replaced it with personal autocracy.'[20] Later, after she had sent a letter to David Owen criticising Alliance defence policy, Mr Steel said: 'You would think she is trying to treat us as though we were members of her Cabinet.'[21]

The Labour Party, too, hammered the 'over-mighty' theme. In a radio interview Neil Kinnock described Mrs Thatcher as a practitioner of 'one person government',[22] though, as he explained later, it wasn't entirely her fault as 'the sycophants and assorted doormats' around the Cabinet table allowed her to get away with it.[23] Labour's most barnacled figure in the then Shadow Cabinet, Denis Healey, emerged from port like a long mothballed Dreadnought to declare it was 'a matter of legitimate public concern that she is concentrating power in No. 10 Downing Street and in a most dictatorial way'.[24]

The achievement of yet another three-figure majority brought no respite from this. Like a spectre at the feast, as Mrs Thatcher celebrated in the opening days of 1988 her surpassing of Asquith's record as the longest-serving premier of the century, her former Defence Secretary, Sir John Nott, delivered himself of the most explosive fusillade since his successor at Defence, Michael Heseltine, had made her style of government the centre-piece of his lengthy resignation statement over Westland.[25] 'The full Cabinet', Sir John said in a *Panorama* interview, 'was *never* more than a rubber stamp' (emphasis added). He spoke too of a 'cult of personality'.

But most devastating of all – and to some it will amount to proof positive – is a remark attributed to Margaret Thatcher herself in Hugo Young's *One of Us*. 'She once told her most senior official adviser', Mr Young wrote in what I took to be a reference to the former Cabinet secretary, Sir Robert Armstrong,

in a moment of speculative candour, that the position she really fancied was that of President not Prime Minister. There was nothing she would like better than to take on the Labour leader, head to head, and beat him into the ground on a national vote. After that, how much more efficient it would be if she exercised something like Presidential powers. It would be a presidency with a difference, of course. A President below a Monarch. But in a perfect world it might enable her to hasten the expunging of Socialism and the remaking of Britain.[26]

That kind of talk makes me shudder as it would whichever Prime Minister of whatever party said it. It stiffens my conviction that the restraint of collective Cabinet discussion should be a crucial check and balance at the very highest level of our public life. But, as I shall indicate, I resisted the temptation to mount a picket at the entrance to Downing Street, in a one man Pilgrimage of Grace, to save the British Constitution. Before explaining why, I must cap the pile of evidence which suggests the problem was real and serious by looking at the resignation of Nigel Lawson as Chancellor of the Exchequer in October 1989.

THE LAWSON RESIGNATION

The Lawson resignation gave us a memorable political autumn in 1989. Like Westland, the personality clash of strong-minded minister against overbearing Premier (of proud man versus determined woman) had been building up for some time with, in this case, the presence of a third figure – Sir Alan Walters – flying in regularly from Washington to put everyone's nerves on edge. Once more it was the European dimension that put the final match to the tinder.

Put aside the matter of who said what to whom, whether Alan Walters should have been allowed to write his biographical article for the *American Economist* and whether he said anything new when he did, the issue boiled down to this: did collective Cabinet government fulfil the function the Constitution requires of it? The answer is an unequivocal 'no'.

Let me explain. Ours is a system without maps. It is built on convention, precedent, procedure, not on a set of written constitutional principles such as most nations feel the need to have. It's almost as if, in George Dangerfield's words, successive generations of British politicians and public servants had shrunk from 'conjuring' our 'great ghost' of a constitution 'into the narrow and corruptible flesh of a code'.[27] This being so we depend on a system of institutionalised checks and balances to protect us, the citizenry, from arbitrary or capricious government. Of these the two most important are an effective Opposition in Parliament and a genuine and consistent exercise of collective responsibility within the Cabinet room. For collective Cabinet responsibility is the key coolant in the engine room of central government, the *only* guarantor against an over-heated premiership.

The best intelligence we have suggests there was no proper discussion of currency policy in the European context in the Cabinet room before the Lawson resignation. Indeed the former Chancellor said as much in the House of Commons on 31st October. Listen to his words:

> a key question is where the exchange rate fits in [to economic policy]. Is it to be part of the maximum practicable market freedom or is it to be part, indeed a central part, of the necessary financial discipline? I recognise a case can be made for either approach. No case can be made for seeming confusion or apparent vacillation between these two positions.
>
> Moreover, for our system of Cabinet government to work effectively, the Prime Minister of the day must appoint ministers that he or she trusts and then leave them to carry out the policy.
>
> When differences of view emerge, as they are bound to do from time to time, they should be resolved privately and wherever appropriate collectively.[28]

You don't have to work at GCHQ to decode that. The message was 'in clear' and in two parts: (1) membership of the exchange rate mechanism was an appropriate subject for collective resolution in Cabinet; (2) it had not been so resolved.

Now you could get cynical at this point on two counts. First, Mrs Thatcher's colleagues only became constitutionally sensitive when they had lost. It's as if they stormed out of the Cabinet Room and wrapped themselves in the folds of A. V. Dicey to clothe personal pique in dignified raiment. There is something in that. Secondly, what guarantee is there that if there had been a collective discussion on the European Monetary System the result would have been any different?

It could be argued, correctly, that Mrs Thatcher didn't have to 'count the voices', that she could sum up in her own favour against the opinion of the undoubted majority, thereby precipitating Lawson's departure irrespective of the side-show of the economic consequences of Sir Alan Walters.

Here I call in evidence Lord Hailsham. Lord Hailsham, doing a marvellous 'I was there' impression, told the viewers of BBC Television's *On the Record* on 5 November that before the famous Treasury resignations in January 1958 there had been exhaustive Cabinet discussion of the issue which divided Peter Thorneycroft and his junior ministers, Enoch Powell and Nigel Birch, from Cabinet thinking as a whole. He's right. I consulted the Cabinet minutes. Cabinet Secretaries always take an especially full note when a resignation threatens.[29] Sir Norman Brook certainly went to town at the two Cabinet meetings on 'Government Expenditure' on Friday 3 January 1958[30] and the final meeting on Sunday 5th at the end of which:

> The Chancellor of the Exchequer said that he had never wavered in his view that Government expenditure in 1958–59 should not substantially exceed the level in 1957–58 and that, although he was well aware of the difficulties entailed by some of the measures to this end which he had proposed, he must now consider his own position in the light of the Prime Minister's summary of the issues at stake.[31]

Now, I don't know – can't know – if Nigel Lawson would have stayed had the Cabinet discussed the issue as fully as Macmillan's Cabinet did in January 1958. What I do know is that the aftermath would not have been the hugely messy and protracted business it was. Whether with a full Cabinet discussion behind her Mrs Thatcher could have got away with dismissing the Lawson affair as 'a little local difficulty'[32] as Macmillan managed to do with the Thorneycroft resignation, I don't know; I doubt it. But it strikes me that she got the worst of all worlds and she deserved to.

Why? Because she simply could not admit there was a problem with her style. In interview after interview she said it was her way and she wouldn't change. And, if her *Panorama* interview on 27 November is a guide, she really had managed to convince herself that her way was the collective way. Listen to this: 'Yes, I do lead from the front. Yes, I do have fundamental convictions. . . . But we do have very lively discussions because that's the way I operate . . . then we reach collective decisions, that's collective responsibility.'

Back now to the bigger picture, the whole picture that built up in the Thatcher decade.

The final layer of evidence I must put together from the bits and pieces which make up the physical artefacts of Cabinet government: the committees, the papers, the procedures. Here, too, is evidence of a siphoning-off of collective briefing and discussion. Full Cabinet meetings under Mrs Thatcher were down by nearly a half. Rarely did the Cabinet meet more frequently than once a week. Cabinet committees, too, were spawned at about half the pre-1979 rate. As for Cabinet papers, these were down by 1989 to about 60 a year, about one sixth of the standard annual flow since the war.[33] Much more business was conducted in informal *ad hoc* meetings which do not figure in the Cabinet Office's committee book. Quite often a paper was prepared for such a group which, likewise, doesn't figure in the Cabinet paper tally. On such occasions Mrs Thatcher, the document before her glowing with 'high-lighted' passages, interrogated the hapless minister whose responsibility the subject matter was before proceeding to act as judge and jury in her own cause.[34] She developed the habit, too, of chairing occasional seminars (an excellent idea, I reckon) on such themes as the 'Greenhouse Effect', football hooliganism or the future of television, at which those involved in the business (not football hooligans, I hasten to add) were invited to No. 10 to kick around an issue with the PM and her ministers.

NOT AN OVER-MIGHTY PREMIERSHIP?

All in all, the charge sheet of an over-mighty premier riding roughshod over the convictions and customs of collective Cabinet government is pretty impressive even leaving out the singular episode of Westland where just about every canon of the Constitution – Cabinet procedure, official secrecy, the *Pay and Conditions of Service Code* of the civil service – was flouted.[35] The question remains: does each particle filling-in bit by bit a wider canvas actually add up to a true picture which, in melodramatic nineteenth-century style, we might encaption 'The Death of Cabinet Government' and hang in the Tate Gallery?

I think not. There's a lot in it, plenty to worry about, but the colours are not that primary, not quite that stark. Let me tell you why. First, the nature of much of the evidence presented by the case for the prosecution is soured by the acid of catharsis as those Mrs Thatcher removed for one reason or another have sought to heal their wounds by telling us just how terrible it was serving in the trenches under her command. Occasionally, too, there has been more than a trace of the revenge motive. All very human and understandable enough – but these are not disinterested people talking.

However, one departee who I have not mentioned gets relatively close to detachment and his evidence is worth careful weighing. He's Jim Prior, a man, incidentally, whose 'Dear Jim' letter from the PM when he finally resigned in August 1984 was a little gem and brought much harmless pleasure to those who had witnessed the lady in action. 'I take your point about frankness', she wrote. 'That's what Cabinets are for, and lively discussions usually lead to good decisions.'[36] But in his memoir *A Balance of Power* Mr Prior makes it plain that her style in Cabinet, in the first two years of her premiership at least, was substantially different from the conventional wisdom about it: 'In her early years as Prime Minister', he recalled, 'Margaret adhered closely to the traditional principles and practice of Cabinet government. She operated very strictly through the Cabinet committee system with the Cabinet Office taking the minutes.'[37]

There was a crucial exception to this early demonstration of constitutional impeccability, as Mr Prior acknowledges.[38] It was economic policy which was kept firmly away from a Cabinet on whose instincts she could not at that time rely, and this remained the position until the sceptics, outraged at the contents of the harshly deflationary 1981 Budget of which they only became aware at the last minute, kicked up a fuss and obliged the Prime Minister to concede an occasional full Cabinet discussion on economic policy.

On the subject of Jim Prior's memoir, it is worth a quick digression which may explain in part the 'she who must be obeyed' syndrome which so often brought electricity into the antiseptic air of the Cabinet Room. In its way it was an early experience comparable to the one in which her father, Alderman Alfred Roberts, was obliged by the controlling Labour Group to set down his aldermanic robes in Grantham in 1952, 'a tragedy' as she recalled, an event which still brings tears into her eyes when she recalls it[39] and is often held to be the primary source of her animus against local government.

I think Jim Prior has found the Cabinet Room equivalent of that grim experience when he recalls her treatment as Secretary of State for Education and Science during the Heath administration of 1970–4:

> She had always been cold-shouldered by Ted; she sat in Cabinet on his right side, carefully hidden by the Secretary of the Cabinet, who was always leaning forward to take notes. [Macmillan put Enoch Powell in a comparable position on his left because he couldn't stand those staring eyes glaring accusingly at him across the table. Mr Powell, incidentally, has publicly praised Macmillan, of whom he is in general highly critical, for his habit of admitting his political enemies to his Cabinet.[40]] It was the most difficult place for anyone to catch the Prime Minister's eye, and I am sure that she was placed there quite deliberately.[41]

And there's more evidence from the early 1970s which could explain why initially in 1979 Mrs Thatcher didn't want to operate through Cabinet committees at all though, as one insider put it to me, 'events soon took care of that'.[42] Jim Prior again:

> In Ted's government, Margaret had been left out from the *ad hoc* committees which were set up. Any Secretary of State for Education is always stuck in a rather isolated department. She had, however, proved herself a disruptive influence on one Cabinet committee, the Science Committee, where she had complained that Solly Zuckerman [Chief Scientist, Cabinet Office] and Victor Rothschild [Head of the Central Policy Review Staff] were only officials and had no right to speak. They in their turn complained about her.[43]

If you've spent four years in the British ministerial equivalent of a Soviet Siberian power station, found yourself placed in the Cabinet Room equivalent of a coal-hole, been excluded from all the interesting Cabinet committees and then, by a set of curious chances found yourself number one, able to control all the patronage, determine who sits where, and open, close and intervene in any discussion you like, it would be beyond the capacity of the once-deprived flesh and blood not to indulge oneself now and again – and again. If you add to that a burning set of political convictions and the suspicion you're the best, perhaps the only 'man' in the Cabinet, you have all the ingredients for apparent dominance.

Certainly her Cabinet Room style was very different from nearly all the holders of the premiership after Neville Chamberlain. Others have dominated, certainly (just as others, Attlee in particular, have shifted a phenomenal amount of business through Cabinet and Cabinet committee) but they have dominated by less obtrusive means. Mrs Thatcher's style was to open a meeting by saying what she thought in that bell-like voice and almost daring colleagues to defy her. It was all so unlike Churchill, the arch-constitutionalist, who would even let them discuss and decide nuclear weapons policy, or Macmillan with his jokes and historical allusions and his evocations of the trenches in the Great War or the dole queues of interwar Stockton. It was all very different, too, from the shrewd Cabinet management of her immediate predecessor, Jim Callaghan, who knew how to get his way without filling No. 10 with broken bones.

But style, however imperial or presidential (and it's often been that), is not the same as substance. Let us do an exercise based on what the secret services call 'negative intelligence'. Let's look at one or two things that did *not* happen though she would, at one time, clearly have liked them to. It is important to do this because several instances have been quoted – rightly – where she was out of step with the majority of her Cabinet and where she prevailed, most notably on the poll tax – which she was for and they were not – and British participation in the exchange rate mechanism of the European Monetary System, where it was the other way round.

But take Northern Ireland. In the early days she was convinced by the Airey Neave line that a restoration of 'good' local government was what the province needed. The presence of two ex-Northern Ireland Secretaries in the Cabinet, Willie Whitelaw and Francis Pym, was sufficient to remind her that it was the absence of 'good' local government in the first place which had been a major contributor to a re-eruption of the troubles in the late 1960s, quite apart from the difficulty she would have experienced in getting agreement for a revised old-style Stormont through the House of Commons. And, of course, with the Hillsborough Agreement of 1985 her back was turned on that impulse for the foreseeable future.

One could mention three British institutions which would either have gone to the wall or have been altered beyond recognition had her will and her will alone prevailed in Cabinet committees which she could quite easily have convened and packed with her supporters or the wholly supine. British Leyland, I suspect, would not have outlived 1981; the principle of a tax-payer-funded National Health Service free at the point of delivery would have gone by the mid-1980s (and, contrary to what you might think, the principle – I emphasise, the principle – has stayed intact); and I shudder to think what condition my beloved BBC would be in by now if the Whitelaws and the Hurds had not been around to restrain and to argue in private.

Let me give you a good piece of supporting evidence for this. It comes from the very same *Panorama* interview in which John Nott talked about the 'rubber stamp' Cabinet and her 'personality cult'. 'Many of those around her', said Sir John, 'provided very necessary restraint. The number of times when she would possibly have gone over the top without the restraint of her colleagues are too numerous to mention.'[44] This, to me, shows that the key function of Cabinet government remained operational. The real problem, I reckon, was that after the Cabinet purges of 1981 and 1983 it did not operate with sufficient frequency, a position made worse by the retirement in 1987 of that great oil-can of the post-1979 Cabinets, Lord Whitelaw, whose generally unrevealing memoirs corroborate other people's testimony about the frequency and importance of his private words with the PM prior to a potentially fractious Cabinet and Cabinet committee meeting.[45] For the key fact about Cabinet government – and what stopped it from tilting towards prime ministerial government – was the willingness of Cabinet ministers individually and collectively to speak out, speak up, argue and stand their ground whatever the rhetorical barrage flying at them from the Gatling Gun of a premier sitting beneath Walpole's portrait.

When that happened Mrs Thatcher did listen, did take notice and could be deflected. Officials consistently testified to this, in private naturally, and so did her colleagues, especially the most seasoned of them all, Lord Hailsham, who has seen every Tory PM in action since Winston Churchill and, from his father, also had a pretty good idea of how Baldwin and Chamberlain conducted themselves. In 1986 I had the good fortune to ask Lord Hailsham about the Thatcher effect in Cabinet, while he was still a member of it, on-the-record for a television interview. I shall remember for years the wheezing ebullience with which he delivered his verdict:

> I don't think the critics have got it quite right when they say that she doesn't like people who differ from her. She reminds me very much of some judges before whom I've appeared who form their own opinion by arguing with counsel. Now Lord Goddard was one such judge. And you would think for a time he was really against you and had made up his mind that you were wrong before you'd had your say. And indeed if you laid down on your back with your paws in the air and wagged your tail, you'd lose your case. . . . I think the present Prime Minister is somebody who likes to test her steel in real argument and I don't think she holds it against you even if you hit back pretty hard.[46]

My breath was taken away: a Cabinet colleague *defending* Mrs Thatcher by comparing her to the late Lord Goddard, the hardest member of the judiciary in the postwar period – and I said so. 'He was a sweet man', said Lord Hailsham.[47]

When Cabinet ministers were not prepared to treat Mrs Thatcher as Lord Hailsham treated Lord Goddard the key safeguard of the system did not function adequately. When they failed to do so, or rather didn't do so often enough, the system under-performed temporarily. But it was not destroyed. The moment ministers asserted themselves, all cylinders in the Cabinet – the right and proper engine-room of central government – began to fire. That's why some kind of written constitution for Cabinet government, in addition to *Questions of Procedure for Ministers* (the secret volume of 'tips for beginners', as the former Cabinet Secretary Lord Trend called it[48]) would make no difference to its health. It's all down to people – 21 of them – who sit around the Cabinet table with the PM.

Before summing up, in my best judicial manner, I ought to mention another mitigating circumstance in the case *against* Mrs Thatcher. In practical as opposed to constitutional terms, it could be argued that her curbing of discussion, trimming of meetings and culling of paper was her particular solution to the problem of 'overload', as the political scientists like to call it. This phenomenon – of an exhausted Cabinet of overworked ministers trying to do too much and continually overreaching themselves and overstraining the system – has been recognised as a problem for more than thirty years. Shortly before becoming Prime Minister in 1957 Harold Macmillan commissioned a group of privy councillors under Lord Attlee to investigate 'The Burden on Ministers' and to advise him what to do about it. A similar impulse lay behind Ted Heath's *Reorganisation of Central Government* White Paper in 1970.

Mrs Thatcher's assault on the problem, launched characteristically without advice from the Good and the Great or a White Paper, was different and, up to a point, successful. But only, I fear, in the short term. If you streamline the process to the point where you endanger its collective essence you store up problems in the long term (your policy solutions might not endure as long as if they had been bashed about more in Cabinet or Cabinet committee). You also store up problems in the medium term: problems of accumulated resentment which erupt in a Westland crisis or a Lawson Affair, when one important Secretary of State can take no more.

CONCLUSION

In 1989, the tenth anniversary year of that 'sacred day', as a former senior official called it with just a touch of irony in his voice,[49] when Mrs Thatcher won her first majority, I offered my assessment of the health of Cabinet government in Britain. I did so in the original version of this paper, when the foregoing analysis was presented in present rather than past tense. My conclusion, quite simply, was that Cabinet government was peaky but not poorly. It had taken a bit of a hammering since Jim Callaghan left the Cabinet room. At some moments, total nervous collapse seemed imminent, as during the weeks of Westland or the row in Cabinet the morning after the F-111 bombers returned from Libya. But

I estimated then that its powers of recovery were considerable and – as I told my audience in Hull – 'I reckon it will be completed in the few hours between the next Prime Minister (doesn't matter who it is or which party) kissing hands at the Palace and going on television to deliver an address which will start something like this:

> Good evening. As you know I have accepted Her Majesty the Queen's commission to form a government. I want to say one thing to all of you at the outset – one thing that will affect everything I do or say from now on. I believe we are never so strong in this country as when we concentrate on the things which unite us rather than divide us.

And so on. Wholehearted Cabinet government, like Winston in 1939, will be back.' Since saying that, Sir Geoffrey Howe has pushed the plunger to set off the biggest political explosion of recent history. Mrs Thatcher did not survive the blast. The problems that had stored up under her style of Prime Ministerial leadership finally did come home to roost. An 'over-mighty' premier was unable to withstand them. A new Prime Minister has ascended the steps of No. 10, given something like the speech I anticipated and given time and space at the Cabinet table to ministers prepared to speak their mind.[50] Older readers will remember the cardboard notices which appeared in the rubble the morning after the blitz. 'Business as usual' they used to say. That, I said in 1989, would be what it would be like on the first day of the post-Margaret era. John Major can put the sign in his window. I rest my case.

NOTES

1. W. Bagehot, *The English Constitution*, 1867 (London: Fontana, 1963) esp. pp. 59–81.
2. W. Bagehot, *Physics and Politics* (London: Henry S. King, 1872). For the book's genesis see N. St John-Stevas (ed.), *Bagehot's Historical Essays* (London: Dennis Dobson, 1971) pp. x–xi.
3. Ibid., p. 161.
4. It was the kind gift of Rupert Pennant-Rea, Bagehot's current successor in the editorial chair at *The Economist*.
5. J. K. Galbraith, *The Affluent Society* (London: Hamish Hamilton, 1958). Ch. 2 is wholly devoted to 'The Concept of the Conventional Wisdom', pp. 5–15.
6. Bagehot, *Physics and Politics*, pp. 163–4.
7. The interview was published in *The Observer* on 25 February 1979.
8. K. Harris, *Thatcher* (London: Weidenfeld & Nicolson, 1988) p. 79.
9. R. J. Minney (ed.), *The Private Papers of Hore-Belisha* (London: Collins, 1960), p. 130.

10. Conversation with Lord Jenkins, 23 March 1988.
11. Harris, *Thatcher*, pp. 79–80.
12. See N. Wapshott and G. Brock, *Thatcher* (London: Macdonald, 1983), p. 198.
13. N. St John-Stevas, 'Prime Ministers Rise and Fall but the Cabinet Abides', *Daily Telegraph*, 7 August 1986.
14. Lord Soames delivered this verdict to me and it was published non-attributably in P. Hennessy, 'From Woodshed to Watershed', *The Times*, 5 March 1984. Now that he is dead I can, I feel, put his name to it.
15. *Nine O'Clock News*, BBC1, 10 January 1986.
16. *News At Ten*, ITN, 10 January 1986.
17. Mr Walker was quoted in 'Friday People', *The Guardian*, 22 November 1985.
18. Conversation with David Howell, 21 February 1985, for the BBC Radio 3 series, 'The Quality of Cabinet government', quoted in P. Hennessy, *Cabinet* (Oxford: Blackwell, 1986) pp. 95–6.
19. Macmillan was quoted in 'Living Legend who Rocks the Boat', *The Observer*, 17 November 1985. In fact, he had coined the phrase at a private meeting of the Conservative Philosophy Group on 11 July 1983.
20. Quoted in R. Harris, 'Blazing June for High-Noon Thatcher', *The Observer*, 10 May 1987.
21. 'Quotes of the Day', *The Independent*, 22 May 1987.
22. Neil Kinnock interviewed by Peter Murphy of Independent Radio News, 31 May 1987.
23. J. Pienaar and A. Marr, 'Thatcher the Target of More Personal Attacks', *The Independent*, 2 June 1987.
24. Denis Healey on *The Six O'Clock News*, BBC1, 1 June 1987.
25. See P. Hennessy, 'The Cabinet: Progress Report 1988', *Contemporary Record*, 2 (5), Spring 1989, pp. 40–1.
26. H. Young, *One of Us* (London: Macmillan, 1989) p. 324.
27. G. Dangerfield, *The Strange Death of Liberal England* (London: Paladin, 1983) p. 44.
28. 'Parliament and Politics', *The Independent*, 1 November 1989.
29. I am grateful to John Barnes of the London School of Economics for this point.
30. Public Record Office, CAB 128/32, CC (58), 1st and 2nd conclusions, 3 January 1958.
31. Public Record Office, CAB 128/32, CC (58), 3rd conclusion, 5 January 1958.
32. See A. Horne, *Macmillan, 1957–82*, vol. 2 (London: Macmillan, 1989) pp. 61–90.
33. I have written about this elsewhere. See Hennessy, *Cabinet*, pp. 99–101.
34. Ibid., p. 103.
35. For a reconstruction of the Westland affair from a constitutional perspective, see P. Hennessy, 'Helicopter Crashes into Cabinet: Prime Minister and Constitution Hurt', *Journal of Law and Society*, 13 (3), Autumn 1986, pp. 423–32.
36. The exchange of letters was reported in *The Times*, 1 September 1984.
37. J. Prior, *A Balance of Power* (London: Hamish Hamilton, 1986) p. 133.
38. Ibid., p. 119.
39. Young, *One of Us*, pp. 28–9.
40. Lord Home, *The Way the Wind Blows* (London: Collins, 1976) p. 192. I have checked his position with Enoch Powell. For Mr Powell's praise of Macmillan, see E. Powell, 'Harold Macmillan', *Contemporary Record*, 2 (1), Spring 1988, p. i.
41. Prior, *A Balance of Power*, p. 117.
42. Hennessy, 'The Cabinet: Progress Report 1988'.
43. Prior, *A Balance of Power*, p. 133.
44. Hennessy, 'The Cabinet: Progress Report 1988'.
45. W. Whitelaw, *The Whitehall Memoirs* (London: Aurum Press, 1989), pp. 261–5.

46. Lord Hailsham interviewed for Brook Productions' *All the Prime Minister's Men*, 14 May 1986.
47. Quoted in P. Hennessy, 'The Prime Minister, the Cabinet and the Thatcher Personality', in K. Minogue and M. Biddiss (eds), *Thatcherism: Personality and Politics* (London: Macmillan, 1987) p. 55.
48. Quoted in P. Hennessy, *Whitehall* (London: Secker and Warburg, 1989) p. 302. In 1989 I launched a vain attempt to persuade Mrs Thatcher to declassify *Questions*: see P. Hennessy, 'Whitehall Watch: Thatcher Declines to Disclose Rules of the Ministerial Game', *The Independent*, 1 May 1989.
49. Quoted in P. Hennessy, 'Margaret's Mixed Blessings', *The Times Educational Supplement*, 14 April 1989.
50. P. Hennessy, 'Whitehall Watch: War gives Major a new gravitas', *The Independent*, 21 January 1991.

3. Judicial Independence in Britain: Challenges Real and Threats Imagined*

Gavin Drewry

The existence of a judiciary that operates independently of and is protected against improper pressure by the executive is universally regarded in developed democracies as a bulwark of both representative government and the rule of law. This is certainly the case in Britain, notwithstanding the absence both of a codified separation of powers and of a Bill of Rights, and the tardy development of anything remotely resembling a developed system of administrative law. In an age of 'big government' and executive domination of the House of Commons (underpinned by an electoral system whose fairness is widely disputed), the courts seem to some people to offer the only possible check upon the excesses of elective dictatorship and of large-scale, imperfectly accountable public bureaucracies: this view has been implicit, and sometimes explicit, in the debate that has been rumbling on since the mid-1970s about whether Britain should either enact its own Bill of Rights or incorporate the European Convention on Human Rights into domestic law. It should be noted, however, that other observers take no comfort at all from the prospect of non-elected, non-accountable and socially unrepresentative judges – however 'independent' they may be – purporting to check the actions of elected politicians and their officials. The judicial process, according to this view, can never be a substitute for the political process.[1]

This chapter proceeds from the premiss that an independent judiciary (the meaning of the term is considered below) is a good worth fighting hard for; but it goes on to argue that there has in some quarters been a degree of over-zealousness, potentially detrimental to the credibility of the judges themselves, in protesting too much about imagined threats – threats which may reflect nothing more sinister than concern about securing adequate public accountability for increasingly expensive legal services, including those provided through the medium of the courts.

Judicial independence is such a familiar part of our vocabulary that for most of the time we probably give very little thought to it. It has melted into the landscape of political and constitutional discourse. However, discerning readers of British newspapers in the last year or two may have noticed that the phrase 'judicial independence' has recently enjoyed a much higher profile than that to which it has hitherto been accustomed. Recent events have also demonstrated a tendency to use the expression rhetorically, without sufficient thought to what it really means.

This was particularly evident in the aftermath of publication in January 1989 of the Lord Chancellor's three Green Papers on legal services and the legal professions – in particular the one entitled *The Work and Organisation of the Legal Profession*,[2] which proposed relaxing the barristers' long-established monopoly of advocacy in the higher courts, and introducing a new system for licensing advocates. A lay-dominated advisory committee (a reconstituted version of the Advisory Committee on Legal Education, now to become the Advisory Committee on Education and Conduct), would advise the Lord Chancellor 'on the education, qualifications and training of advocates appropriate for each of the various courts. The Lord Chancellor should be required to consult the judiciary before reaching decisions as a result of advice tendered by the Advisory Committee, although the final decision would be for him'.[3]

It confronted the cherished autonomy of the bodies representing the branches of the legal professions, thus:

> Professional bodies whose members wish to offer advisory and advocacy services will be required to submit their proposed codes of conduct for the endorsement of the Advisory Committee whose role it will be to ensure that such codes of conduct embody the approved principles.... The Government proposes that the Lord Chancellor should prescribe by statutory instrument the principles which must be embodied in these codes.... The Government is not prepared to leave it to the legal professions to settle the principles which these codes should adopt because they will be of great importance both to the administration of justice and to the public.[4]

Hereupon, many leading members of the Bar, and senior judges, went on record as saying, often in rather extravagant language, that all this posed a gross threat to judicial independence and the rule of law. In the Lords' debate on the Green Papers,[5] the Lord Chief Justice, Lord Lane, attacked the new advisory committee procedure as a movement towards executive control over the judiciary, adding for good measure: 'Oppression does not stand on the doorstep with a toothbrush moustache and a swastika armband'.[6] Lord Donaldson, Master of the Rolls, said that, if necessary, he would tell the Government to 'Get your tanks off my lawn'.[7] Former Lord Chancellor, Lord Hailsham, said that he was 'shocked' by the prospective threat posed to judicial independence:

> It is proposed in the Green Paper that a member of the executive, advised by an advisory committee which is staffed secretarially by his own department and composed of a majority of persons unqualified in the law, shall be in command of the qualifications, the ethics and the statutory framework within which the right to practise is exercised. That same member of the executive is to be in command of the whole of that apparatus. Where are we going if that is to remain the case?[8]

Part of the answer to Lord Hailsham's rhetorical question is that we are going less far than was originally envisaged because the government watered down various aspects of its scheme in response to some of the objections raised. The clauses in the Courts and Legal Services Bill relating to rights of advocacy provided in effect that before final approval of the rules by the Lord Chancellor, the four most senior judges[9] must also give approval; but a schedule to the Bill said that any such 'designated judge' who declines to approve would be publicly identified, along with his reasons for dissenting;[10] in theory, this could render the judges' veto subject to judicial review in the courts. The judges remained less than satisfied with this and other aspects of the package, but the language of their opposition was much more muted than that used in the earlier debate on the Green Papers. Perhaps it was realised that judicial independence can more plausibly be defended if the judges themselves refrain from descending too noisily into the parliamentary arena.

The bemused observer, brought up in a culture where (in deference to the British model of judicial independence) judicial utterances are seldom contradicted save by other judges, was left wondering if the proposals in their original form really did pose such a serious threat to the constitutional order. Or was hyperbole of the kind just cited from judges and lawyers (and there is plenty more where that came from) simply a self-interested knee-jerk response on the part of an articulate professional pressure group which is very well represented, perhaps over-represented, in Parliament?[11]

At least two other examples come to mind where controversy has arisen over supposed threats to judicial independence. The first is a continuing saga about the management of magistrates' courts. The Justices' Clerks Society and the Magistrates' Association have expressed anxiety about the implications for the independence of magistrates posed by the Home Office's Scrutiny Report (the Le Vay Report) on Magistrates' Courts, published in 1989, which proposed setting up an independent management agency to improve efficiency.[12] Secondly, in a very different context, we have the continuing debate about sentencing policy – where the success of public policy requires co-operation from the judiciary, but where respect for judicial independence is considered to require that ministers express their views on the subject in oblique language. The Lord Chief Justice has strongly resisted any encroachment by the executive into areas hitherto regarded as a matter solely for the courts and has opposed the oft-mooted proposal for some kind of sentencing council. To quote Frances Gibbs: 'he has always resisted attempts by officials to draw him into discussion on [sentencing] policy; indeed he was recently reported to have left the room during a private Home Office seminar for those involved in the criminal justice system when sentencing came up.'[13] This is in rather striking contrast to the episode a few years ago when *Time Out* was the grateful recipient of a leaked memorandum relating to an interview between Lord Donaldson and the newly appointed permanent secretary to the Department of Employment, Michael Quinlan, who apparently wanted some advice about industrial law reform. The wrath of the establishment fell upon the leaker rather than upon the judge.[14] However, there is evidence in the archives of the Lord Chancellor's Department that suggests that this episode is far from unique.[15] It can of course be argued that this kind of dialogue between judges and administrators should be welcomed rather than condemned; but the judges cannot blame critics for commenting adversely upon episodes of this kind given that they themselves get so worked up about their independence from the executive. Moreover, present attitudes encourage judges and civil servants to converse covertly, even furtively, rather than openly – a fact which further inflames outsiders' suspicions.

What then is the meaning of this familiar phrase 'judicial independence', in defence of which so many strong words have been uttered?

JUDICIAL INDEPENDENCE

It must be noted at the outset that the notion of judicial independence is linked to other concepts, in particular those of impartiality and neutrality. We must be careful not to confuse them.

Independence has to do with the absence of improper external pressures and with the capacity of judges to resist such pressures without fear of penalty. In so far as the concept is historically bound up with the constitutional doctrine of separation of powers (and several of the critics of the Mackay Green Papers expressly alluded to that doctrine) the 'improper pressures' referred to are principally those that may emanate from the Executive and from Parliament. However, the realities of modern corporatist government demand a wider definition. To quote Simon Shetreet:

> Independence of the judiciary has normally been thought of as freedom from interference by the Executive or Legislature in the exercise of the judicial function. . . . In modern times, with the steady growth of the corporate giants, it is of the utmost importance that the independence of the judiciary from business or corporate interests should also be secured. In short, independence of the judiciary implies not only that a judge should be free from governmental and political pressure and political entanglements but also that he should be removed from financial or business entanglements likely to affect, or rather *to seem to affect him* [see below], in the exercise of his judicial functions (emphasis added).[16]

Then we have the related, but quite distinct, concept of *impartiality* which, to quote John Bell, 'involves the judge listening to each side with equal attention, and coming to a decision on the argument, irrespective of his personal views about the litigants' – this being the essence of the phrase, 'equality before the law'.[17] *Neutrality* requires that 'whatever his personal beliefs, the judge should seek to give effect to the common values of the community, rather than any sectional system of values to which he may adhere'.[18] Bell goes on to note that, while there may be some connection between the ideas of impartiality and neutrality, 'there is no reason why the reputation of judges for being willing to listen to all sections of the community should necessarily depend on them adopting a politically neutral position'.[19]

At this point it should be noted that all these concepts have a subjective as well as an objective quality. It is crucial for the authority of the courts and for the legitimacy of the processes by which justice is administered, that people *believe* in the independence, the impartiality and the neutrality of judges. And it is in this subjective dimension of the subject that the boundaries between these logically quite different concepts is apt to become blurred. One can readily understand, for instance, how a perception – justified or not – on the part of, for instance, trade unionists, ethnic minorities and women that the judicial process, operated almost exclusively by middle class, white males, is working in a partial way, and to their detriment, might also foster doubts about the claims of judges to being politically neutral. This in turn may well encourage a belief that judges whose political neutrality is suspect *might* be less independent, in the sense of being immune from outside political influences, than they like to pretend. This muddying of definitional waters has been a feature of political rhetoric about judges; for instance, in the context of the debates in the early 1970s about the role of the Heath Government's National Industrial Relations Court, and of the more recent controversies about the desirability or otherwise of introducing a Bill of Rights.

Meanwhile, the link between independence and impartiality is the basis of an interesting account of judicial independence, in W. A. Robson's pioneering, *Justice and Administrative Law*. Robson starts from the premiss that impartiality is a fundamental prerequisite of justice. He then proceeds to argue that such impartiality requires an independent judiciary, noting that, in Britain, independence has came to be associated with security of tenure:

> Whether or not the decisions of a judge bring satisfaction or anger to the Prime Minister and his colleagues, or to the Lord Chancellor, he cannot be dismissed at will. His tenure is for life, or until retirement, subject only to good behaviour. His salary is fixed and paid out of the Consolidated Fund in order that it may not be subject to that running fire of criticism in Parliament to which all the ordinary items of budgetary expenditure are liable. His conduct cannot even be discussed in Parliament save on a substantive motion for an address for removal from office: an extreme step to be taken only in the event of impropriety of the gravest kind. The judiciary is, in effect, part of the public service of the Crown. But a judge is not 'employed' in the sense that a civil servant is employed. He fills a public office, which is by no means the same thing; and part of his independence consists in the fact that no one can give him orders as to the manner in which he is to perform his work.[20]

However, Robson also makes the important point that tenure is not a *logical* prerequisite of independence: 'judges might be appointed for a set term of years ... and administrative officials might be appointed for life subject only to good behaviour; and no immediate change might be perceptible in the method of carrying out their duties'.[21] The importance of tenure for judicial independence is psychological: unlike the administrator, the judge

> can displease an indefinite number of persons an indefinite number of times without any personal consequences ensuing to himself, providing only that he remains sane and does not commit one of those enormities which constitute misconduct. ... The independence of the judge is ... of essential importance in so far as it enables the judge to adopt a particular attitude of mind towards the questions which come before him for decision. He can, in short, determine the case before him without fear that adverse results or material reward will accrue to him according to whether the decision does or does not meet with the approval of other persons.[22]

Writing more recently,[23] Rodney Brazier has suggested four prequisites for judicial independence:

1. Judicial appointments and promotions should not be subject to uncontrolled ministerial patronage.
2. Judges should be free from improper attempts by ministers, MPs or peers to influence the results of cases still under adjudication.
3. Judicial salaries should not be reduced.
4. Judges should not be removed from office unfairly or without reason.

He goes on to argue that existing arrangements broadly satisfy the last three conditions – but he argues that there are serious problems with the first. His article is, in essence, a critique of the Lord Chancellor's exercise of patronage, of the secrecy surrounding the operation of the Lord Chancellor's Department and of the absence of satisfactory machinery to secure public accountability for legal services. Brazier calls for the creation of a new 'Department of Law' (thus carefully avoiding the provocative term 'Ministry of Justice').

THE OFFICE OF THE LORD CHANCELLOR

In theory the main custodian of judicial independence in England is that peculiar constitutional animal, the Lord Chancellor, who guards the frontier between government, the judiciary and Parliament, being himself a member of all three branches; a minister who presides, nowadays, over a large departmental empire of about 11,000 civil servants, with an annual budget that approaches £1bn. In recent years, that empire has absorbed, and become increasingly absorbed by, the familiar watchwords of Thatcherite public administration: efficiency, effectiveness and economy; value for money; market forces; contracting-out public services; Raynerism; the Financial Management Initiative, and so on. This, as we shall see, raises issues that are highly germane to the subject of this chapter.

But meanwhile the Lord Chancellor remains, constitutionally, a member both of the executive and of the judiciary. And the supposed importance of retaining the Lord Chancellor's position as constitutional link-man between the two branches of government, in order to safeguard judicial independence was stressed by Lord Chancellor Birkenhead, in an essay published in 1922:

> if they are totally severed there will disappear with them any controlling or suggestive force exterior to the Judges themselves, and it is difficult to believe that there is no necessity for the existence of such a personality, imbued on the one hand with legal ideas and habits of thought, and aware on the other of the problems which engage the attention of the executive government. In the absence of such a person the judiciary and the executive are likely enough to drift asunder to the point of a violent separation, followed by a still more violent and disastrous collision.[25]

Later Lord Schuster, the permanent secretary of the Department throughout the interwar years, was to refer in a departmental memorandum to the need for 'some link or buffer' between executive and judiciary;[26] later still, his successor, Sir Albert Napier,[27] used the metaphor of a constitutional 'hinge' to describe the Lord Chancellor's position. This remains the conventional wisdom of today: thus Sir Nicolas Browne-Wilkinson, Vice Chancellor of the Supreme Court (and so destined, coincidentally, to become one of the four 'designated judges' of the Courts and Legal Services Bill), in a public lecture delivered at Lincoln's Inn in November 1987[28] referred to the unique constitutional position of the Lord Chancellor as providing 'a flexible and efficient means to transmit the needs of the legal system to the executive and to Parliament'. Lord Mackay himself quoted the above passage from Lord Birkenhead's essay, with evident approval, in his recent Earl Grey Public Lecture.[29]

Which takes us back to those debates on the 1989 Green Papers: 'tanks on the lawn', 'swastika armbands' and all that. A degree of creative tension between the different branches of government is arguably a healthy and inevitable feature of mature democracy, but this sort of language, directed by senior judges at the minister responsible for the judiciary, and himself a judge *ex officio*, suggests that the buffer may have broken, that the hinge badly needs oiling and that something may have gone wrong with Sir Nicolas Browne-Wilkinson's 'flexible and effective' means of transmission.

THE LORD CHANCELLOR: PROBLEMS AT THE CONSTITUTIONAL VORTEX

The Lord Chancellor does have one advantage denied to his ministerial colleagues: he is required to be an expert in the main subject of his department's business. But his multiple role in superintending/appointing the judiciary, safeguarding its independence from Executive interference, and answering to Parliament for the machinery of justice, entails a heroic piece of stagecraft, one which requires in turn a massive suspension of disbelief on the part of the spectator.

The main criticisms are well known. First, it has long been a matter for adverse comment that the Lord Chancellor does not sit in the Commons; the Attorney General (who has no power to command the officials of the Lord Chancellor's Department and has a job that is quite different from that of the Lord Chancellor) deputises for him. He acts 'as a courier between the Commons and the Lord Chancellor – and indeed as a courier who rarely brings any reply'.[30] Secondly, his relations with the judiciary are highly secretive, and the manner in which his powers of discipline, patronage and promotion are exercised has given rise to intermittent concern. Robert Stevens has culled some lurid episodes that bear upon this in his trawl of the files of the Lord Chancellor's Department, cited earlier.[31]

Let us pause to consider just one aspect of this: the removal of members of the higher judiciary on a formal address – something that has not actually happened since 1830.[32] Paterson and Bates have pointed out that no Scottish or English judge has ever actually been removed in modern times. Not, they rather cryptically suggest, 'because there have not been any unfit or incapable judges during that time' but because:

The perceived importance of the separation of powers and the independence of the judiciary is such that successive Lord Chancellors and Lord Presidents have preferred to put pressure – sometimes very strong pressure – on judges to resign rather than to invoke more formal measures. Since 1890 there have been at least 15 instances where judges of the superior courts in the United Kingdom have been the subject of strong pressures or inducements to resign, ostensibly on the grounds of ill-health which they were reluctant to face up to or incapable of recognising.[33]

And, they go on:

The problem with such an approach is not just the secrecy with which it is pursued but that it provides no overt support for the democratic principle that public officials who are entrusted with considerable powers should be held accountable for the exercise of these powers.

There is a third area of difficulty, perhaps the trickiest of all. The JUSTICE report on the Administration of the Courts (published in 1986 and considered more fully below) looked at the problem of how best to handle public complaints against judges. The report says that some members of the Committee believe that the increasing tendency for public authorities to be involved in litigation will make it 'increasingly difficult for the public to accept that judges are independent when the head of the judiciary, who is responsible for their behaviour, is also a leading member of the government'. One solution, they suggest, would be to restrict the role of the Lord Chancellor to being head of the judiciary and Speaker of the House of Lords – which 'would be a logical solution if as some have suggested, a Ministry of Justice is set up, with its departmental Minister in the House of Commons'. This possibility is tentatively mooted but the report stops short of making a positive recommendation along these lines.

THE SPECTRE OF EXECUTIVE CONTROL: DEBATE ABOUT A MINISTRY OF JUSTICE

Others have not been so reticent. Since the Haldane Report on the Machinery of Government in 1918[34] there have been various proposals from various sources for a rejigging of ministerial responsibilities for the machinery of justice and for the establishment of some kind of Ministry of Justice.[35] Some recent variants of this have surfaced in policy documents from the former Alliance parties[36] and from the Labour Party which, in its 1990 policy review document, has called for a new Department of Legal Administration;[37] Brazier, as we have seen, takes a similar position. There has been little consistency in the proposals put forward – and indeed the ground has shifted over the years. Since the 1940s, for example, changes in the arrangements for judicial business in the House of Lords have made it much harder for Lord Chancellors to find time to sit judicially. And since the early 1970s the Lord Chancellor's Department has grown from a tiny domain concerned mainly with judicial patronage, into a major spending department with about 11,000 civil servants, responsible for administering a major public service.

One common ingredient in these proposals has been that the Minister of Justice should sit in and be accountable to the House of Commons. Another common factor has been that whenever the phrase 'Ministry of Justice' has been mentioned there has been an almost audible shudder of horror from the judges about the supposed threat such a development would pose to their independence. Lord Chancellor Hailsham (while claiming, himself, to be a Minister of Justice[38]) made clear his own fierce resistance to developments of this kind: he said of the Alliance's proposal for a new Department of Justice that such a move would be 'constitutionally very dangerous' and a menace to the independence of the judiciary.[39]

Since Lord Hailsham's departure from the office of Lord Chancellor, the spectre of executive inroads into judicial independence has been raised in a new context – and with a new villain in the shape of Lord Chancellor Mackay, an outsider to the cosy traditions of the English Inns of Court and a proponent of a utilitarian-Thatcherite outlook on the machinery of justice, very different to that of his predecessor – and author of those three famous Green Papers discussed earlier.

THE BROWNE-WILKINSON THESIS

However, this part of the story begins in the Hailsham era, and not so much with the Green Papers themselves but with the cult of efficiency and economy that has been such a feature of the Thatcher years. The Lord Chancellor's Department, like every other department in Whitehall, has become subject to the new disciplines of Raynerism and the Financial Management Initiative (FMI). The Civil Justice Review (initiated by Lord Hailsham),[40] the reorganisation of legal aid and the Green Papers are all products of this.

Sir Nicolas Browne-Wilkinson, the Vice-Chancellor of the Supreme Court, foreshadowed some of the anxieties articulated by the judges in the context of the Green Paper debates in his 1987 public lecture, cited earlier.[41] Writing before the Green Paper debates but anticipating, in measured language, some of the shriller protests of his judicial colleagues, Sir Nicolas identified several developments in the last thirty years or so that, in his view, posed a threat to the continuing independence of the administration of justice.

He noted, for instance, the post-1971 shift in the administrative control of the courts from judges to civil servants in a Lord Chancellor's Department that has undergone a considerable expansion since the Second World War. Noting that the theoretical distinction between administrative and judicial functions is not so easy to maintain in practice as some might like to pretend, he suggested that this has 'given rise to stresses between the judiciary and the administrators as to their different functions'.[42] The administrative listing of cases for trial is a notoriously vexed illustration of this point. There has recently been a running saga over the exclusion of the Parliamentary Commissioner from reviewing alleged maladministration on the part of court staff who, although they are civil servants, act, at least theoretically, under the instruction of judges.[43] Sir Nicolas pointed to worrying deficiencies in the command structure, in that there is no machinery for resolving disputes between judges and administrators, short of the Lord Chancellor himself.[44]

The point on which he laid greatest stress has to do with the recent development of Financial Management and Value for Money disciplines relating to public expenditure, and their application to the Lord Chancellor's Department:

> the requirements of judicial independence make the Lord Chancellor's Department wholly different from any other department of state. It is not for the executive alone to determine what should be the policy objectives of the courts. It is not for the executive alone to determine whether or not a particular judicial procedure provides 'value for money'. Justice is not capable of being measured out by an accountant's computer ... [U]nder our constitution it is for the judge to determine what is just, and what is not just, subject always to legislation passed by Parliament. As a result of such policy being applied to the Lord Chancellor's Department, that department is being required to formulate policy and to make determinations as to 'value for money' according to financial yardsticks and without, for the most part, even consulting the judges.[45]

Thus, said Sir Nicolas:

> The Lord Chancellor's own position, representing as he does simultaneously both the independent judiciary and the interests of government, is becoming more and more difficult, since the price to be paid for obtaining funds for the administration of justice is dependent on satisfying the Treasury that any particular course represents, in their terms, value for money.[46]

His Department is forced by the demands for financial economy to move more and more into areas which the judges have traditionally considered to be their exclusive preserve.

While conceding that 'there is no justification for a claim that the legal system has a greater right to public funds than, for example, the National Health Service or education',[47] he went on to argue that, while the fixing of the total budget must be a political act, judges must, in the interests of judicial independence, be involved in the preparation of the estimates and in the allocation of the budget once it has been voted by Parliament. By the same token, judges should be more involved in the formulation of legal policy. Sir Nicolas concluded, first, that the dual role of the Lord Chancellor should continue; secondly, that 'there should be a collegiate body of judges charged with responsibility for taking policy decisions on behalf of judges': funded by the Lord Chancellor's Department but accountable to the Lord Chancellor for its expenditure of those funds.[48]

Even if we accept Sir Nicolas's diagnosis it is hard to see how the latter proposal could be made to work in practice. Consultation is one thing, 'responsibility' is very much another. Lord Mackay in the Earl Grey public lecture referred to earlier[49] seems implicitly to reject this plea for direct judicial involvement, certainly in respect of funding matters, while at the same time defending his own position as a minister in the House of Lords:

> The House of Commons is not itself a policy-making body. In such a system, the judicature needs a minister to act as its friend at court [an interesting phrase], who can compete on equal terms – so far as differences in size permit – with other spending departments for a share of the public money. The intensity of political conflict in the House of Commons also makes it desirable, in our system, that the judiciary should not become directly involved in the politically charged process of obtaining resources. The Lord Chancellor serves to insulate them from that process.

So now we have the metaphor of 'insulation' to set alongside those noted earlier, such as the 'buffer' and the 'hinge'.

We have already noted the colourful language used by senior judges in the context of the debates on the 1989 Green Papers. The issues were aptly summarised in an *Observer* article, published soon after the Lords' debate, which noted the unbridgeable gap

> between those who believe that legal services (which are largely paid for out of the Exchequer) should be subjected to empirical tests of efficiency and accessibility, and those who believe that the present disposition of the English legal system was brought down from Sinai by the framers of the Revolution Settlement and should not be tampered with by outsiders.[50]

Readers may by now have begun to suspect, quite correctly, that the author of this chapter is emphatically in the former category. A legal system exists to provide a service to the public. Judges seem sometimes to forget that they are paid public servants and to give the impression that defending their constitutional fortress against the theoretical possibility of attack takes priority both over quality of service and value for money. An independent judiciary seems all too often to be depicted as a self-evidently admirable end in itself rather than as a means to an end.

The same tendency on the part of judges to close ranks and to rail, sometimes in intemperate language, against any attempts to impose even a modicum of external quality control, has bedevilled the debate about acccountability for legal services, to which I now turn.

PARLIAMENT, JUDICIAL INDEPENDENCE AND THE DIVISION BETWEEN 'JUDICIAL' AND 'ADMINISTRATIVE' FUNCTIONS

Here we take it for granted from the outset that the machinery of justice is a part (albeit a peculiar part) of the apparatus of government, and that the administration of justice is an important public service (as well as being an expensive one, subsidised by the taxpayer). This may seem so obvious as hardly to be worth saying, but it seems that some lawyers do sometimes need to be reminded of it (witness the debates on the Green Papers). The 1986 JUSTICE report on *The Administration of the Courts* put it thus:

> The courts exist for the benefit of the public and provide, and should be seen to provide, a public service, as much as, say, the National Health Service. We would like to see a wider recognition of this fact. The customer in the law

courts may not always be right but it is he or she, and not the judges or lawyers, for whom the service is provided.[51]

Opening the Commons debate in July 1979 on motions to establish a new system of departmentally-related select committees, Norman St John-Stevas rejected a proposal by the Procedure Committee[52] that the Home Affairs Committee should undertake scrutiny both of the Lord Chancellor's Department and the Law Officers' Department. In his speech (prompted, as it has since been made clear, by Lord Hailsham) St John-Stevas spoke of the threat to the independence of the judiciary that might arise

> if a select committee were to investigate such matters as the appointment and conduct of the judiciary and its part in legal administration, or matters such as confidential communications between the judiciary and the Lord Chancellor and the responsibility of the Law Officers with regard to prosecutions and civil proceedings.[53]

He added that the Lord Chancellor's functions are all 'deeply interwoven with judicial matters'. But, as several Members pointed out, it simply isn't true to suggest that judicial independence is threatened by committee investigations into the administration of, for instance, legal aid (or for that matter the Public Record Office). It seems clear that the Procedure Committee never envisaged the Home Affairs Committee looking at judicial activity as such.

Both the Home Affairs Committee and the Liaison Committee have pressed the government to change its mind, so far without success. And, in the meantime, Lord Hailsham voluntarily gave evidence to the Home Affairs Committee both in its Prisons inquiry and its Remands in Custody inquiry , and the British constitution apparently remains more or less intact; the English and Scottish Law Officers have also given evidence to the Committee. In any case, the Lord Chancellor's Department has always been answerable to the Public Accounts Committee.[54]

Lord St John of Fawsley has since explained that the exclusion was a matter of tactics[55] but John Wheeler, chairman of the Home Affairs Committee, has broadly accepted the Hailsham line, arguing that 'to some extent the lack of direct monitoring of the Lord Chancellor's Department has been justified by the need to preserve judicial independence'.[56] This is one of many instances of a widespread tendency to be very protective – arguably over-protective – towards the judiciary when it comes to public accountability. Another is to be found in the 1986 JUSTICE Report, cited earlier.[57]

THE 'JUSTICE' REPORT ON THE ADMINISTRATION OF THE COURTS

The Committee that produced this report was set up, under the chairmanship of John Macdonald QC, to inquire into the machinery for dealing with public complaints about the administration of the courts. The inquiry excluded consideration of complaints about the merits of courts' decisions (in respect of which there is often a right of appeal), and time and time again the report comes back to the need to preserve judicial independence by separating 'administrative' matters from 'judicial' ones – a division that Sir Nicolas Browne-Wilkinson (see above) has acknowledged to be highly problematical.

Thus the report discusses the role of the Parliamentary Commissioner for Administration who in 1984 reached a concordat with the Lord Chancellor's Department about the location of the boundary line between 'administrative' and 'judicial' (a matter best left, the JUSTICE committee argues, in another part of the report, to the 'common sense' of experienced LCD officials), since when 'the number of complaints involving the Department has risen'. The 1984 agreement subsequently broke down following the Lord Chancellor's Department's obtaining counsel's opinion to the effect that court staff supplied by the LCD but working under the instructions of judges did not come within the purview of the Parliamentary Commissioner Act 1967: and the Select Committee on the PCA took evidence on the subject from both Lord Hailsham and Lord Mackay.[58] The Lord Chancellor subsequently agreed to bring his Department within the purview of the PCA by way of a new clause in the Courts and Legal Services Bill.

The Committee also notes the rather startling fact that, in dealing with complaints by disgruntled litigants, the Lord Chancellor's Department's refusal to accept responsibility for administrative actions carried out on the instructions of a judge has meant that only 5 per cent of complaints are accepted for consideration. It says, with some understatement, that it is not surprising if such a low take-up rate gives rise to 'some lack of confidence' in the system.[59]

In fact, the Committee – in common with so many other people – became preoccupied with the issue of judicial independence to a point where it virtually lost sight of any legitimate claims of public account-ability. At one point it considered the objections that might be raised to extending the powers of the PCA to include investigations of judicial behaviour, a change favoured by some members of the Committee. One objection, it said, 'is that, as the Ombudsman reports to the House of Commons, this would *encourage MPs to pry into the affairs of the judiciary*' (emphasis added).[60] But this objection was then promptly rejected on the grounds that the PCA is an independent officer who 'would only investigate a complaint if he were satisfied that it was serious', and, the Report continues, 'if a serious complaint is made, it would seem better that it should be investigated by an independent person of the standing of the Ombudsman than for it to become *the subject of ill-informed speculation in Parliament*' (emphasis added).[61] So much for parliamentary accountability: no wonder parliamentary discussion *is* sometimes ill-informed given the prevalence of this kind of thinking.

CONCLUSIONS

Judicial independence is, as William Robson argued, an important precondition for impartiality (a necessary condition, though not a suffi-cient one); both attributes have a subjective as well as an objective dimension. This writer does not dispute for one moment that issues like judicial patronage, salaries, removal from office are of historical impor-tance, and he shares much of the concern of Brazier and others about the defects in the present departmental arrangements pertaining to the administration of justice, and about the secrecy and lack of accountabil-ity pertaining thereto. We should also recognise that the judges – notably Sir Nicolas Browne-Wilkinson – have a point when they say that the terms of their old partnership with the Lord Chancellor, acting traditionally as a constitutional 'buffer' in defence of their independence, have altered significantly, and probably irreversibly, as the LCD has become more and more like any other large spending department, imbued with the tough managerial values of the Thatcher era and fighting its corner with other departments for scarce public resources.

But in any case, the subject goes far wider than the traditional boundaries of judicial independence set out in standard textbooks on constitutional law. The formal buttresses of judicial independence – removal only on an address, salaries directly chargeable to the Consolidated Fund, and so on – are virtually worthless if the self-professed independence and impartiality of judges are doubted by those whom the courts are there to serve. An emphasis upon the impartial quality of the judicial process, with the justification of independence recognised as being its role in underpinning impartiality and a recognition of the subjective quality of these attributes, brings much more sharply into play a number of issues that might be regarded as peripheral if we were confining ourselves to the issue of whether judges really are manipulated by the executive – issues such as the method of appointment and the judges' social/educational backgrounds.

It is quite possible (as United States Presidents have sometimes found to their surprise) for judges who owe their offices to political patronage to display robust independence once they are in post. The proclaimed end of a political spoils system (from the late 1920s) in Britain is commonly regarded as having been an important watershed in enhancing the *perceived* impartiality of the judiciary – though there is no evidence that judges appointed in the 1920s were any more or less 'partial' than their successors. Indeed, because of the secretiveness of the Lord Chancellor's Department and the cliquiness of the Bar there is not a lot of evidence of any kind relating to judicial appointments, promotions, and so on: a booklet on the subject of appointments produced by the LCD is a singularly unrevealing document.[62]

Can the public, whose taxes pay judicial salaries, be blamed if it, and its elected representatives, sometimes wonder what the profession has to hide? Similarly, judges have been inclined to scoff at the notion that their impartiality might somehow be compromised by the narrow exclusiveness of their social and educational backgrounds. Perhaps they are right; but secretiveness is the enemy of informed discussion, and in any case they surely cannot blame people for musing upon the implications of, for instance, the Bar's long-held monopoly of judicial appointments and of the almost total absence of women and ethnic minorities from the professional Bench.

Public perceptions of the judiciary, and confidence in the judicial process itself, must surely be influenced for the worse by their exclusiveness, their defensiveness, their complacency[63] and their propensity to attack their critics with stridently expressed constitutional platitudes in lieu of reasoned argument – the Green Paper debates are a case in point. The problem is exacerbated by lack of parliamentary accountability and by the secrecy surrounding matters pertaining to judicial appointments. The Courts and Legal Services Act 1990, with its emphasis on the interests of the consumers of legal services, is in principle to be welcomed rather than rudely dismissed as a threat to judicial independence. The latter, as defined earlier in this chapter, remains an important constitutional principle, but discussion of it cannot be conducted without due regard to far wider issues relating to the judges and the judicial process – and to the nature and funding of legal services in a modern democracy.

NOTES

*   The original version of this paper was delivered (as mentioned in the editor's preface) as a seminar paper in the Department of Politics at the University of Hull (November 1989); a later version was delivered as a public lecture at the Centre for British Constitutional Law and History, King's College, London, in February 1990. Preparation of the final version of the chapter has taken grateful account of comments and suggestions made on those two occasions. Several paragraphs of the chapter also appeared in my inaugural lecture, 'Never Mind the Administration, Feel the Justice', delivered at Royal Holloway and Bedford New College on 3 May 1990.

1. Notably J. A. G. Griffith, 'The Political Constitution', *Modern Law Review*, 42, 1979, pp. 1–21.
2. Cm 570, 1989.
3. Ibid., paragraph 5.13.
4. Ibid., paragraphs 4.11-4.12.
5. *House of Lords Debates*, vol. 505, c. 1307–1480.
6. Ibid., c. 1331.
7. Ibid., c. 1369.
8. Ibid., c. 1333.
9. The Lord Chief Justice, the Master of the Rolls, the Vice-Chancellor of the Supreme Court, the President of the Family Division.
10. Schedule 4, para. 11.
11. The Judges are directly represented in Parliament by the Law Lords. During the Lords' Second Reading debate on the Courts and Legal Services Bill (*House of Lords Debates*, 19 Dec. 1989, c. 154), Baroness Phillips noted that of 36 peers who had put their names down to speak, 28 had been trained as lawyers. In the Commons about 100 MPs are lawyers, two-thirds of them barristers.
12. ' "Efficiency Role" for New Magistrates' Courts Agency', *The Times*, 20 July 1989; see also the editorial in *New Law Journal*, 28 July 1989, p. 1029; and J. Davis, 'A Water-Tight Case for Court Overhaul', *The Times*, 26 September 1989.
13. *The Times*, 5 February 1990.
14. See R. Pyper, 'Sarah Tisdall, Ian Willmore, and the Civil Servants' Right to Leak', *Political Quarterly*, 56, 1985, pp. 72–81, and the editorial comment, 'Secrets, Moles, Ministers and Judges', *Public Law*, 1984, pp. 173–7.
15. R. Stevens, 'The Independence of the Judiciary: the View from the Lord Chancellor's Office', *Oxford Journal of Legal Studies*, 8, 1988, pp. 222–48.
16. S. Shetreet, *Judges on Trial* (Amsterdam: North-Holland, 1976) pp. 17–19.
17. J. Bell, *Policy Arguments in Judicial Decisions* (Oxford: Clarendon Press, 1983) p. 4; cf. W. A. Robson, *Justice and Administrative Law*, 3rd edn (London: Stevens, 1951) p. 369.

18. Bell, *Policy Arguments*, p. 4.
19. Ibid.
20. Robson, *Justice and Administrative Law*, pp. 43–4.
21. Ibid., p. 45.
22. Ibid., pp. 46 and 48.
23. R. Brazier, 'Government and the Law: Ministerial Responsibility for Legal Affairs', *Public Law*, 1989, pp. 64–94, at p. 74.
24. There is a large literature on the office of the Lord Chancellor: an excellent bibliography can be found in P. Polden, *Guide to the Records of the Lord Chancellor's Department* (London: Lord Chancellor's Dept, 1988).
25. Viscount Birkenhead, *Points of View*, vol. 1 (London: Hodder & Stoughton, 1922) ch. 4.
26. Public Records Office, file LC02 3630.
27. Public Records Office, file T162 877/E48680, 1944.
28. Sir N. Browne-Wilkinson, 'The Independence of the Judiciary in the 1980s', *Public Law*, 1988, pp. 44–57, at p. 45.
29. Lord Mackay, 'The Role of the Lord Chancellor in the Administration of Justice', Earl Grey Lecture, University of Newcastle, 24 February 1990.
30. Brazier, 'Government and the Law', p. 68.
31. Stevens, 'The Independence of the Judiciary'.
32. Shetreet, *Judges on Trial*, pp. 143–4.
33. A. Paterson and St John Bates, *The Legal System of Scotland*, 2nd edn (Edinburgh: Green, 1986) p. 172.
34. ICd 9230, 1918, ch. X.
35. See G. Drewry, 'Lord Haldane's Ministry of Justice – Stillborn or Strangled at Birth?', *Public Administration*, 61, 1983, pp. 396–414, and 'The Debate about a Ministry of Justice – A Joad-Eye's View', *Public Law*, 1987, pp. 502–9.
36. 'Government, Law and Justice: the Case for a Ministry of Justice', *Alliance Papers No. 1* (London: SDP/Liberal Alliance, 1986).
37. *Looking to the Future* (London: Labour Party, 1990) p. 40.
38. Fourth Report from the Select Committee on Home Affairs, *The Prison Service*, Session 1980–81, HC 412 (London: HMSO, 1981) Evidence, QQ 995–6.
39. *Guardian*, 26 May 1986.
40. *Report of the Review Body on Civil Justice*, Cm 394, 1988.
41. Browne-Wilkinson, 'The Independence of the Judiciary in the 1980s'.
42. Ibid., p. 46.
43. See n. 58 below. Also the Parliamentary Commissioner for Administration, *Annual Report for 1988*, 1988–89, HC 301, para. 60, and JUSTICE report, *The Administration of the Courts* (London: JUSTICE, 1986), paras 2.20–2.24, 3.7–3.9 and Appendix D.
44. Browne-Wilkinson, 'The Independence of the Judiciary in the 1980s', p. 47.
45. Ibid., pp. 48–9.
46. Ibid., p. 50.
47. Ibid., pp. 53–4.
48. Ibid., p. 56.
49. Mackay, 'The Role of the Lord Chancellor in the Administration of Justice'.
50. L. Mark, *The Observer*, 9 April 1989.
51. JUSTICE report, para. 3.1.
52. First Report, 1977–78, HC 588, para. 5.24.
53. *House of Commons Debates*, 25 June 1979, c. 35ff.
54. For a recent instance, see Sir Derek Oulton's evidence to the Public Accounts Committee, 9 April 1986, 1985–86, HC 182.
55. Second Report from the Select Committee on Procedure, *The Working of the Select Committee System*, Session 1989–90, HC19-II (London: HMSO, 1990), para. 742.

56. Letter to *The Times*, 16 February 1989.
57. JUSTICE Report, *The Administration of the Courts*.
58. Evidence of Lord Hailsham, 31 March 1987, 1986–87, HC 284-ii; evidence of Lord Mackay, 26 January 1989, 1988–89, HC 159.
59. JUSTICE Report, *The Administration of the Courts*, para. 3.7.
60. Ibid., para. 4.14.
61. Ibid.
62. *Judicial Appointments: The Lord Chancellor's Policies and Procedures* (London: Lord Chancellor's Department, 1986).
63. The recent record in relation to the courts' reluctance to face up to past mistakes in respect of gross miscarriages of justice might be cited under both the last two headings.

4. The Changing Face of Parliament: Lobbying and its Consequences

Philip Norton

Constituents and groups making representations to ensure that their views are heard or their demands met – in short, lobbying – is a well-established feature of American politics. It is an activity protected by the First Amendment right to petition government for a redress of grievance. In Britain achieving a redress of grievances is a historic task of Parliament, one established within the first two centuries of its emergence.[1] However, lobbying of Parliament has not been a significant feature of British politics in the twentieth century. What lobbying has taken place has been directed at the executive and has been conducted on an institutionalised and essentially private basis. Only in recent years has there been a notable and observable change in practice. Since 1970, and more especially in the past ten years, Parliament has been a target of lobbying. Professional lobbying has become a marked feature of the political landscape. So too has lobbying by constituents. This change has had a significant impact on parliamentary deliberation, both in committee and in the chamber. The purpose of this chapter is to identify the extent of the growth in lobbying, the reasons for it, and the impact it has had upon parliamentary debate.

PARLIAMENT AND POLICY

Parliament is essentially a policy-influencing, or what Mezey has characterised as a reactive, legislature.[2] It has not been a policy-making body on any continuous basis during the seven centuries of its existence. The last occasion when it exhibited some of the characteristics of a policy-making body was for a period of less than 40 years in the nineteenth century. That period was brought to an end by the creation of a mass electorate (by 1884 a majority of working men had the vote) and the consequent development of organised, mass-membership political parties.[3] Party served as the essential conduit for the transfer of power from Parliament to the Cabinet. By the turn of the century, Cabinet dominated the policy cycle. The principal measures of public policy were agreed by the Cabinet – a party-dominated body, headed by the party leader as Prime Minister – and then presented to Parliament for approval. A loyal party majority then ensured the passage of those measures.

By the turn of the century party cohesion was a marked feature of parliamentary life.[4] It remained so. By 1965, Samuel Beer was able to declare that cohesion was so close to 100 per cent that there was no longer any point in measuring it.[5] Candidates were chosen by 'selectorates' and then elected, or not elected, on the basis of their party labels. They became dependent both for campaign organisation and for funding on the party.[6] Once elected, they loyally supported their leaders in the division lobbies of the House of Commons, not so much because they felt they had to but, in most instances, because they wanted to. 'MPs', as one of their number observed, 'have a predisposition to vote for their party, otherwise they would not be there.'[7] On those occasions when they felt uneasy about the position taken by their own party, they were constrained from voting against their own side, in part for fear of what may happen to them (lack of preferment for ministerial office, retribution from the local party) and in part because of a lack of information to pit against that marshalled by ministers. As government developed, qualitatively as well as quantitatively, the House of Commons remained an essentially amateur body meeting in plenary session to discuss those measures which government brought forward. It had neither the time nor the resources to subject increasingly complex and numerous bills to sustained and informed scrutiny. The position was one which suited government. It had no wish to be challenged by the House and so initiated no major change in parliamentary structures and procedures. The one exception was at the beginning of the century, when the referral of Bills to standing committees (unless the House voted otherwise) became standard practice. The move favoured government: more Bills could be considered at the same time. The committees themselves were anything but 'standing': they were appointed *ad hoc* on each occasion a Bill was sent to committee, as still remains the case. They were thus unable to build up a body of permanent expertise. MPs remained 'gifted amateurs'. Until 1911 they were not even paid a salary.

In the four stages of the policy cycle identified by David Olson (those of gestation, preparation, deliberation and implementation), Parliament is thus a central actor – as it has been for most of its history – in only one: deliberation. Party has served to ensure not only that it remains essentially a deliberative body but also to shape and limit the effect of the deliberation that it undertakes. Parliament discusses, but it then approves. Government has been able to proceed in the knowledge of what the outcome will be.

The development largely responsible for the enlargement of the electorate in the nineteenth century was industrialisation. The emergence of a non-landed middle-class excluded from the franchise generated demands for change. Industrialisation also generated a more complex and specialised society. Interests became more differentiated and increasingly organised. Pressure groups – making irregular or consistent demands of government, without themselves seeking to form the government – grew in number and prominence. Government itself became increasingly dependent upon such groups, especially sectional interest groups, for information, for advice and for co-operation in the implementation of policy. This dependence has been pronounced in the case of Britain, given the nature of the groups. Sectional interest groups, unlike many of their equivalents in the United States, have often achieved a monopoly or near-monopoly of expertise in their particular sectors, as actual membership has come close to potential membership. 'If doctors are as powerful', Rudolf Klein noted, 'it is not just because of their characteristics as a pressure group but because of their functional monopoly of expertise.'[8] Such groups were drawn increasingly into the early stages of policy development. Indeed, a number were effectively co-opted into the process. On occasion, that co-option was provided for by statute. Thus, for example, the National Health Insurance Act of 1924 provided for the functional representation of specific interests, such as the medical profession, on various committees appointed to administer the system of social insurance. Analogous provisions had appeared in the Trade Board Acts of 1909 and 1918. Such statutory co-option expanded throughout the century, especially after 1945 and the development of the welfare state and the managed economy. By 1978 more than 1500 advisory bodies and more than 500 similar bodies with executive powers existed; various groups enjoyed representation on such bodies, either as of right (granted by statute) or by the exercise of ministerial discretion. In the 1960s and 1970s tripartite bodies – drawing together representatives of government, labour and business – grew in number: these included the National Economic Development Council, the Health and Safety Commisssion and the Manpower Services Commission.

Such bodies constituted the formal tip of an iceberg. Government departments maintained close and regular contact with groups in their sectors of responsibility. Such contact usually took place between civil servants in the appropriate functional unit of a department and the representatives of groups operating in their area. One of the characteristics of the British policy style, according to Richardson and Jordan, is that of 'bureaucratic accommodation'.[9] There is a desire within each of these policy communities to reach agreement. Disputes could threaten the relationship established between civil servants and groups and pass the problem on for others to resolve. The relationship has thus been a consensual one. Once agreement is reached, the proposal is then 'sold' to the rest of the department, percolating upward for ministerial approval. Only in a very few cases will it get as far as the Cabinet. There has thus been an extensive, institutionalised process of incremental policy-making taking place in a growing number of small policy communities, that process being largely shielded from the public gaze.

In this process Parliament has played little or no part. Once a department has been persuaded of the need for change there is little else for a group to do. Where parliamentary approval is required the government's majority delivers it. In presenting the measure the government will emphasise the extent to which it is an agreed package, the product of consultation with affected groups. For pressure groups, lobbying Parliament has thus not been seen as necessary. When indulged in it has been taken as an admission of failure, resorted to only when attempts to influence the relevant department have failed. Utilising the institution as a 'second-best' channel of influence has been a characteristic especially of promotional groups advancing causes for which government has little sympathy or on which it has adopted a neutral position. Parliament has been an arena in which a number of social issues have been debated, not always without effect,[10] but it has not been the target of regular and extensive lobbying by a wide range of pressure groups. Indeed, for most established interests, Parliament – and especially parliamentary procedure – has been a closed book.

Members of Parliament before the 1970s were thus rarely troubled by lobbyists – professionally or otherwise; indeed there were hardly any of the former. Nor were they overly troubled by constituents. Increasing government involvement in the social and economic life of the nation generated a greater number of citizen grievances. MPs sought a redress of such grievances. As such, they became more constituency-active than before.[11] However, the demands were not overly onerous. In the 1960s an MP received on average between 20 and 100 letters a week, mostly from constituents. Though holding constituency 'surgeries' (being available at specific times to see constituents) became common practice, there was no requirement to live in the constituency. Some MPs made what were rare visits to their seats; some found that they could reply to letters in longhand; and devoting considerable time to constituency matters – earning the appellation of 'a good constituency member' – was generally equated with being a failed minister.[12]

For MPs the overwhelming point of reference in parliamentary activity remained that of party. The chamber was the arena for the clash between the two main parties, allowing for what Bernard Crick characterised as a 'continuous election campaign'. Members were essentially cocooned by party; parties determined electoral outcomes; and outside pressures – from groups, from individual citizens – could usually be resisted with relative ease.

A LOBBYING EXPLOSION?

Since 1970 there has been a significant and observable change in parliamentary lobbying. There has been a modest qualitative change; it is now more professional. There has been a major quantitative change; there is now extensive and continuous lobbying of Parliament. The growth in lobbying activity is not confined to a particular type of lobbying nor to a particular source. The past twenty years have witnessed an expansion in three principal types of lobbying:

Professional lobbying

Before 1970 there were virtually no professional lobbyists – those offering for hire their services to pinpoint and exploit relevant contacts in Whitehall and Westminster. Professional lobbyists – and firms of lobbyists under the nomenclature political consultants – began to emerge in the late 1970s and more especially in the 1980s. There is no register or association of such firms and there is a fairly frequent regrouping as personnel are poached or firms merged; consequently no precise figure exists of the number of such groups. However, at least 30 now exist.[13] They are supplemented by a range of individuals, often MPs' research assistants, offering their services. These constitute the independent operators. Many major firms and pressure groups have their own in-house lobbyists: British Petroleum, for example, is particularly well served.

Parliament does not constitute the exclusive focus of such consultants. It does, however, constitute 'in most cases ... a major and visible focus'.[14] Consultants are variously hired on a long-term basis to help raise the profile of groups among Members of Parliament. On other occasions they may be hired on a short-term basis to mount what are known as 'fire brigade' campaigns to influence the provisions of particular bills. During the passage of the Financial Services Bill in 1986, for example, consultants retained by institutions in the City of London were especially active. A 1985 survey of 180 sizeable companies found that more than 40 per cent utilised the services of political consultants.[15] Their use extends now to many promotional groups.

'Amateur' lobbying by groups

Many groups lobby Parliament without engaging the services of political consultants. A survey of almost 350 groups in 1986 found that one-fifth of them hired consultants; however, three out of four had regular or frequent contact with one or more MPs.[16] Of those maintaining such contact, one in three provided information or briefings to all or a large number of Members. (Professional lobbyists by contrast tend to focus on a small number of targeted Members.) Regular contact often takes the form of printed material – newsletters, magazines and briefing documents – while lobbying on particular issues is often done through letter-writing campaigns. Personally written letters usually receive replies from MPs; printed letters are normally 'filed' in wastepaper baskets. The amount of circular material received from outside groups is now substantial; at least one MP keeps a large plastic bin-liner in which to file it. 'Amateur' lobbying will tend to reach a peak when contentious issues are discussed.

Lobbying by constituents

There has been a significant increase in the contact that takes place between constituents and their Members of Parliament. Most of the personally written letters received by MPs still come from constituents. Members now receive in one day the number of letters they used to receive in one week.[17] They spend more time on constituency activity – and, indeed, spend more time in their constituencies[18] – and write an increasing number of letters themselves to ministers in pursuit of constituency casework. MP-to-minister correspondence was substantial by the early 1980s; during the decade it showed a further remarkable growth. In January 1982 approximately 10,000 letters were written by MPs to ministers, mostly on behalf of constituents; in January 1989 the number was 15,000.[19] Most such activity is undertaken on behalf of individual constituents or particular groups within the constituency. On occasion it is the result of a national campaign organised through local supporters. The most spectacular recent example of such a campaign was that conducted against the 1986 Shops Bill, a government Bill to liberalise the law on Sunday trading. Various groups opposed to the Bill, including the Church of England, hired professional help and utilised supporters in the constituencies to put pressure on MPs at local level. The tactic proved stunningly effective. No less than 72 Conservative MPs voted against the Bill, sufficient to ensure its defeat.[20]

Lobbying of Parliament is thus extensive. Professional lobbying is now, relative to the position before the 1970s, big business.[21] Lobbying firms regularly advertise their services. 'Amateur' lobbying by groups – and by constituents – takes place on an even greater scale. The volume of such lobbying continues to increase and is a growing cause of concern. In part the concern is a practical one: how can the limited resources of individual MPs, and of Parliament collectively, cope with the pressure? In part it is also an ethical one: does lobbying by particular groups, especially those utilising political consultants, give them an unfair advantage in terms of access to Westminster and Whitehall? Parliamentary concern has been reflected in two enquiries undertaken into the subject by the Select Committee on Members' Interests – its second report, following evidence taken from a range of political consultants, commentators and political scientists, is scheduled to appear in 1991 – and by an inquiry undertaken by the Select Committee on Services, which looked at problems associated with access to the Palace of Westminster and recommended stricter control on the use of passes to the Palace.

There is a growing debate as to the effect of lobbyists and, if there is a problem associated with their activities, precisely what the problem is. According to some, it is the undue influence they are able to exert on the political system (democratic accountability); according to others, it lies not in the relationship between lobbyist and politician but between the lobbyist and the client (consumer accountability) – civil servants and MPs are well able to resist the blandishments of lobbyists if they wish to; it is the organisation wanting to lobby Parliament which has no idea of who to utilise for the purpose which needs some protection. In terms of prescription, much of the discussion revolves around the introduction of a Register of Lobbyists, though the extent to which that would encompass the mass of 'amateur' lobbying is far from clear. Few proposals are put forward that would actually reduce the volume of the lobbying that takes place. And that volume increases year by year.

EXPLANATIONS FOR THE GROWTH IN LOBBYING

Why has there been such a growth in the volume of parliamentary lobbying? There is no mono-causal explanation. Indeed, it is possible to identify seven plausible explanations – four external to Parliament and three internal – for the growth in lobbying by pressure groups.

The growth in the number of pressure groups

There has been a significant growth in the number of pressure groups in the past 20 to 30 years. Of the groups listed in one directory of pressure groups published in 1979, approximately 40 per cent had come into being since 1960.[22] The increase in numbers, especially in promotional groups, one assumes would have an effect on the volume of parliamentary lobbying; even if groups continued to treat Parliament as a 'second-best' forum for lobbying, the growth in the number of groups would produce an increase in such lobbying.

The shift from distributive to redistributive policy

As the economic conditions of the nation worsened in the 1960s and 1970s – output growth in manufacturing from 1973 to 1978 was actually a minus figure (-0.9 per cent) – so government had to pursue redistributive rather than distributive policies. Those organisations and groups seeking a share of the increasingly limited resources thus had to compete with one another for those resources. That competition generated greater lobbying, principally of government, but, if government proved unresponsive – as demands could no longer be met on the same scale as before – then groups turned their attention to Parliament; such attention remained an admission of failure on the part of the groups, but at least it constituted one more course to pursue.

Government autonomy in policy-making since 1979

The Conservative government, first returned in 1979, has sought to roll back the frontiers of the state and to introduce a market economy. In order to achieve that, the old collectivist methods of policy-making have had to be attacked and disbanded. Government has necessarily had to achieve autonomy in policy making in order to impose its prescription for national recovery. As a consequence, Britain has witnessed the emergence of a strong state and a distancing of government from outside groups, especially peak organisations (such as the Trades Union Congress and the Confederation of British Industry) previously involved in tripartite organisations such as National Economic Development Council (NEDC). Though this distancing has not been as great as many observers have assumed (policy adjustments through policy communities remains the norm), the perception by groups that government is less responsive to group demands has propelled them more toward Parliament as a secondary channel of influence.

The emergence of political consultants

Firms of political consultants have become more numerous as companies and pressure groups have turned their attention toward Parliament. In part, this growth is almost certainly a response to demand. However, it is also likely that it is, in part, supply-led. The availability of consultants has sensitised groups to the value of lobbying and consequently many groups have employed the services of such consultants. Firms of consultants draw their personnel from a range of political activity: journalists, civil servants, parliamentary researchers, party officials and politicians (some firms employ ex-MPs, others retain as advisors serving Members).[23] This expertise has helped entice commercial firms and pressure groups to make use of their services. The more professional help has been employed, and the more it appears to have had some effect, the greater the enticement to others to follow suit in making use of lobbyists.

Behavioural changes in Parliament

Since 1970 the House of Commons has witnessed a notable behavioural change: MPs are more independent in their voting behaviour. The change is relative – party remains the near-exclusive determinant of voting behaviour – but it has been sufficient to prevent government from assuming that it has an automatic majority for whatever it wishes to have passed.[24] In the 1970s successive governments suffered defeats as a result of their own backbenchers voting with the Opposition.[25] In the Parliaments since 1979 there have been some defeats of government but most influence has been exerted through the threat of defeat or the threat of extensive dissent by government backbenchers; government has acted in advance of the issue reaching the floor of the House.[26] Similar behavioural independence has been displayed in the Upper House: peers have continued to impose defeats on the Thatcher government (more than 120 since 1979), with the government either having to accept such defeats or trying to use a Commons majority to overturn them. As a result of this greater, albeit still limited, independence, parliamentarians are more relevant targets than before for those seeking to influence government policy.

Structural changes in the House of Commons

Since the late 1970s the House of Commons has introduced a number of structural and procedural reforms. The most extensive and best-known reform has been the introduction of departmentally related Select Committees 'to examine the expenditure, administration and policy in the principal government departments ... and associated public bodies'. Introduced in 1979, the committees cover almost all government departments. (The exceptions are the Law Officers' Department and – since 1987 – the Scottish Office.[27]) Each committee comprises 11 backbench MPs; no ministers or Opposition front-benchers serve on them. Each committee usually meets once a week and takes evidence from relevant bodies – ministers, civil servants, academics, affected groups – in public session. Each committee determines its own agenda and will normally publish a report with recommendations at the conclusion of each inquiry; the evidence taken in the course of the inquiry is also usually published. The Committees have been very active and certainly very prolific: in the first Parliament of their existence they issued 193 reports and in the Parliament of 1983–7 they issued no less than 306. For groups outside

Westminster the committees have acted as magnets. Groups focus their attention on them, submit evidence to them (be it solicited or unsolicited) and may even be invited to send representatives to appear for questioning before the Committee. By approaching a Committee, a group may be able to persuade it to take up an issue – one that government may have little interest in or time for – and hence get the issue on to the agenda of public debate. By being invited to submit evidence, groups are able to get their views on the public record through the medium of an authoritative public body. The Select Committees thus have the capacity to fulfil important agenda-setting and tension-release roles. Consequently, they are showered with memoranda by groups operating in their sector of responsibility.

The televising of parliamentary proceedings

The House of Lords, following a much earlier experiment, allowed the television cameras to begin recording proceedings in 1985. The House of Commons in 1988 voted to allow the cameras in and the televising of Commons' proceedings began on 21 November 1989. The introduction of television has proved popular with the watching public (in the US as well as Britain) and has added to the attractiveness of Parliament as a focus for lobbying. By raising an issue an MP or peer may attract the attention of the cameras and hence give the issue a wide public exposure. For groups that exposure may be especially valuable in helping to attract popular support and hence increase pressure on government. In order to achieve that, therefore, parliamentarians have to be contacted and persuaded to raise the issue. Hence the greater attractiveness to groups of both Houses of Parliament.

These explanations are complementary rather than competing. They serve to explain the rise in group lobbying of Parliament. The increase in lobbying by constituents has different causes. The increase may be ascribed principally to an increase in constituents' demands and, on the supply side, to a greater professionalism on the part of MPs. Constituents, as we have noted, made greater demands of MPs in the 1960s; those demands increased in the 1970s and 1980s as more citizens were affected adversely by the increase in redistributive policy. Aspiring politicians seeking safe seats were expected increasingly to live in their constituencies; the number of letters written to MPs by constituents increased significantly. This increase in demand coincided with an increase in supply. More MPs than before sought out constituency grievances and made more effort to be seen in, and pursuing the interests of, the constituency. 'Knights of the shires' on the Conservative side – sitting in the House almost as a public duty (for many, a part-time public duty) to discuss affairs of state – and working-class Labour MPs (often former trade union officials given a seat as a reward for past services or as a consolation prize for not achieving high union office) were replaced increasingly by well-educated politicians keen to ascend the ministerial ladder.[28] Constituency service constituted an important part of the job, a means through which a reputation may be made and new candidates in particular were trained in the use of local media (especially local radio – of which older Members had little understanding or experience – and 'freesheets': local papers financed by advertising); such activity may also have been spurred – and may be spurred even more in the future – by some evidence that it garners an electoral reward to a much greater extent than was previously assumed to be the case.[29] An increase in lobbying by constituents thus appears to be both demand- and supply-driven and shows little sign of receding.

EFFECT ON PARLIAMENTARY DELIBERATION

What effect has the increase in lobbying in recent years actually had on parliamentary deliberation? As we have seen, there is a down-side in that it has placed a strain on parliamentary resources; there is a growing danger of parliamentary overload, though lobbying constitutes only one of the contributory variables.[30] There is, though, an up-side in terms of the effect on deliberation, both in committee – especially in committee – and on the floor of the House.

Standing Committees

After the House of Commons approves the principle of a Bill (Second Reading), the Bill is sent to a Standing Committee for detailed considera-tion. (Some major measures of constitutional import, as well as some which require a speedy passage, are taken in Committee of the Whole House.) Each Committee comprises between 16 and 50 Members; the present practice is to appoint 18 members for most Bills. As with all committees, members are appointed in proportion to party strength in the House. Ministers and whips are appointed to each Committee and government and Opposition members sit facing one another. Each Bill is considered on a clause-by-clause basis, amendments being considered before each clause is considered on a 'stand part' motion ('That the clause stand part of the Bill'). The Committees are not empowered to hold evidence-taking sessions and cannot, as Committees, receive evidence from outside bodies; if an outside organisation sends material to the clerk of the Committee with the request that it be circulated to members of the Committee, the material is either returned or discarded. Proceedings in practice have tended to be extensions of the partisan debate that has taken place on Second Reading. In order to expedite proceedings, government backbenchers are encouraged to take vows of silence; in order to delay proceedings, in the (usually forlorn) hope of forcing concessions, Opposition members speak frequently. Even if Committee members wanted to adopt a more critical, bi-partisan approach to the particular provisions of a Bill, they have been constrained by limited information; they have rarely been in a position to challenge the evidence presented by the minister.

The capacity of Standing Committees to scrutinise a Bill effectively is thus limited and has been the subject of several proposals for change. In 1980 the House introduced a provision allowing the appointment of Special Standing Committees, Committees which could hold up to three evidence-taking sessions before reverting to normal Standing Committee format. The first such Special Standing Committee – on the 1981 Criminal Attempts Bill – proved successful. Since then only four other Bills have been referred to SSCs. Despite the House in 1986 changing the rules for moving for the appointment of an SSC (allowing any Member – not just a minister – to move for referral), no Bill has been sent to an SSC in recent years. Various other proposals for change have emanated from the Select Committee on Procedure, but no significant reform has been implemented.[31]

On the basis of this evidence it would be fair to conclude that Standing Committees constitute largely ineffective mechanisms for the detailed scrutiny of government Bills. In practice the position is not quite so bleak. In part this has been because of the behavioural changes noted earlier; since 1970 there has been a greater willingness by Committee members to impose defeats on the government in Committee. This was especially so in the 1970s,[32] but to some extent has been maintained since. What has facilitated the continuation of such independence, and produced a greater degree of critical scrutiny, has been the lobbying of Committee members by outside organisations and pressure groups.

Lobbying of members of Standing Committees is now extensive. The 1986 survey of sectional and promotional groups found that more than 80 per cent of the respondents had been concerned by legislation before Parliament in recent years.[33] Of the groups, almost 60 per cent circularised all or some members of the relevant Standing Committee. More than 50 per cent asked MPs to table amendments. The more organised and persistent groups will hire lobbyists or ensure that some of their own representatives are present throughout committee proceedings and will maintain contact with sympathetic members. Committee members can nowadays often be seen slipping out of the committee room for consultation with group representatives. Some groups organise meetings for Committee members – in 1986, for example, the Stock Exchange provided a briefing session at the Exchange for Labour members of the Standing Committee on the Financial Services Bill – and will send in briefing material to individual members at appropriate points in the Committee proceedings. According to one member of the Committee on the Financial Services Bill, the material that came in 'was a couple of feet thick and may have amounted to a couple of hundred letters and documents'; during the Committee's deliberations more than 80 references were made to group representations – among them the Stock Exchange, the Consumers Association, the Institute of Chartered Accountants, the Law Society of Scotland, the Association of British Insurers, individual companies and even the New York Stock Exchange.[34] The representations were directed at specific provisions, usually seeking some substantive amendment or suggesting some improvement.

The Financial Services Bill was by no means exceptional. Of the Bills considered each year by Parliament (about 60 government Bills), only a small number constitute what may be termed measures of high partisanship. Most Bills go through without a vote on Second Reading and the main provisions of each constitute the means for achieving an end; there is thus considerable potential for improving the specifics of a measure. Briefing material from outside groups has provided a much greater opportunity for Committee members to involve themselves in Committee deliberations. Such involvement has produced greater cross-party agreement. The Financial Services Bill serves again as a useful example: on a number of amendments, two Conservatives joined with Labour Members to produce a majority against the government, while at least one Labour MP on the Committee conceded that he had been influenced by the various representations and discussion in Committee, coming closer to the government's view on one of the Bill's provisions.[35] Such cross-party agreement can produce a sympathetic government response without the threat of defeat. Ministers can prove persuadable on the merits of the argument. This was true during most of the committee stage of the Financial Service Bill in 1986 and, more recently, during the committee stage of the 1990 Broadcasting Bill. As a result of the arguments advanced from both sides, ministers variously accepted substantive changes to the Bill.

The effect of lobbying has thus been to improve the knowledge of committee members and to limit the government's capacity to rely on a party majority to approve automatically whatever it wishes approved. Even when government has stood firm, material furnished by groups has been put to good effect by Opposition members in forcing ministers to justify their position. By utilising contact with Committee members, pressure groups are thus able to ensure a response from government – it helps to get their own view on the public record and induces an authoritative response to it. As a result, groups generally have a positive view of their attempts to influence legislation. In the 1986 survey of pressure groups, a majority of respondents (55 per cent) judged their efforts to influence legislation to be 'very' or 'quite' successful; only 6 per cent judged their efforts to be unsuccessful.[36] For groups and Committee members there are thus benefits to be derived from lobbying activity.

The greater lobbying of Committee members by outside groups may thus be seen to contribute to the fulfilment of the essential function of committee stage – in the words of Erskine May, to render a bill 'more generally acceptable' – and the entry of the television cameras to committee rooms has also given Committee deliberations an added impetus: Conservative members are less willing to take vows of silence. Against this, though, substantial problems remain. Of those groups that seek to influence legislation, most can be characterised as being modestly effective but notably inefficient: most pressure groups are not well-versed in how to target relevant MPs.[37] There is also a divide between those groups who do seek to influence legislation and those that would like to but do not know how or basically lack the resources to do so. Those groups that can hire political consultants to monitor Committee proceedings are better placed to have some influence than those who cannot afford such assistance. And at the end of the day the government can usually rely on its party majority to get its way. However, relative to the position that existed before the 1970s, the deliberations of Standing

Committees have assumed greater relevance in influencing the content of public legislation.

Select Committees

The departmentally-related Select Committees of the House of Commons were established, as we have seen, in 1979. Most of their time is taken up with taking evidence from two categories of witnesses. One comprises those drawn from government: ministers and civil servants. Subjecting ministers and their officials to sustained questioning helps to elicit information that would otherwise be unavailable; it also helps keep departments sensitive to parliamentary reaction. The second, and most numerous, category comprises representatives of outside organisations and pressure groups. Whenever it determines a topic for enquiry, a Committee – through its clerk – will make public the topic and will circulate notification to interested parties. Committees maintain a mailing list of such bodies and will usually invite them to submit written memoranda. A few are likely to be invited to give evidence before the Committee.

The extent to which Committees draw upon evidence from groups outside government is shown in Table 4.1. As the figures demonstrate, ministers and civil servants constitute a minority of the witnesses interviewed by the committees. Oral evidence is given on the basis of invitation. However, any group can submit a written memorandum. As a result some committees are inundated by material from outside groups; on occasion the number will be in three figures. (As yet, though, no departmental Select Committee has received in the course of a single

Table 4.1   Number of witnesses appearing before departmental Select Committees, 1983–7

Witnesses	1983–4	1984–5	1985–6	1986–7
Ministers	49	63	58	40
Civil servants	357	392	380	236
Other witnesses*	1011	1019	925	634

* Includes representatives of public bodies
SOURCE Memorandum of Evidence presented by the Clerk of the House to the Select Committee on Procedure, Session 1989–90, appendix (d).

inquiry the number of memoranda received by the House of Lords Committee on Laboratory Animals Protection: more than 900.[38]) The record so far is held by the Transport Committee which, in the 1987–88 session, received 365 memoranda; the total number received by the departmental Select Committees in that session exceeded 2000. Most come from outside groups, though a substantial proportion emanate from government. Some memoranda constitute no more than letters, others constitute substantial documents outlining considered views or presenting factual evidence. On occasion the Committees will themselves commission some research.

Submitting evidence to Select Committees serves a dual purpose for pressure groups, especially those which have little direct clout with government: it helps get their views on the public record and it allows them the opportunity to try to influence the recommendations of a parliamentary body. Select Committee reports may have some direct and immediate influence on government; following their reports, some action may follow.[39] Failing that, they may serve to provide some new dimension to debate, either in Parliament or among civil servants. According to one former civil servant, even if a report is initially put on the shelf, it is always there to be taken down at a later date by a minister or senior civil servant looking for new ideas.

There is also a value for the committees themselves. Outside organisations provide them with information, thus helping to further their understanding of a particular topic. The organisations also serve to provide advice and analysis which committees can then contrast with that offered by government. In other words, Committees are provided with alternative sources – of advice, of information, of interpretation – to that of government. The existence of the Committees, and their evidence-taking sessions with witnesses other than ministers and civil servants, has contributed to the erosion of the government monopoly of information provided to Parliament.

The relationship between Committees and groups may consequently be described as a beneficial one, contributing significantly to the deliberations of the Committees and putting views and information offered by groups into the public domain. There is little evidence of a 'sweetheart' relationship between particular groups and Committees – in part because of the number of groups operating in each sector and, in part, because of the influence still enjoyed by government (a majority of committee members are government backbenchers) – and little evidence of attempts by groups to use unethical means to influence individual committee members. Where committee members have relevant outside interests these are normally on the public record: the chairman of the Transport Committee even circulated to witnesses details of his outside interests. Nor would there be much point in attempting to exert undue influence on individual members. The Committees are not decision-making bodies – they make recommendations – and a single member would be unable to prevent critical questioning by other members of the Committee. With experience, Committees have become increasingly effective as inquisitorial bodies.

None the less problems remain. The link between the Select Committees and the Floor of the House is a tenuous one. With the introduction of three Estimates Days a session there is now an opportunity to debate some Committee reports, but the vast majority go undebated. Committees have limited resources – they can, and most do, employ part-time specialist advisers, but they cannot always be certain they are getting evidence from the most appropriate sources – and they have limited time: they may only get some of the relevant evidence from witnesses in the time available. Bi-partisanship is a feature of the Committees – they even sit in a semi-circle as opposed to the adversarial format of one side sitting opposite the other – but if an issue becomes contentious there is always the danger of partisanship coming to the fore; knowing this, Committees will often steer away from more contentious issues. Limited time and resources also mean that Committees can investigate only a small number of topics. Hence, for many groups the opportunity to give evidence may rarely occur. And even if a Committee makes a particular recommendation, there is little it can do to get government to act upon it. For formal sanctions a Committee is dependent upon the House itself and there the government can call upon its majority to get its way.

As agents of parliamentary influence, Select Committees are limited bodies. They none the less constitute the most significant parliamentary reform so far this century. They are important scrutineers of government – of government policy and of departmental administration – and in that task they are aided considerably by taking evidence from interested organisations and pressure groups. For committees and groups the relationship is one of mutual benefit.

The Floor of the House

The impact of increased lobbying on the Floor of the House is both direct and indirect. The indirect influence comes through the Select and

Standing Committees. Reports from Select Committees are rarely debated but where relevant to a particular debate they are 'tagged' on the Commons' Order Paper; Select Committee work also produces a number of MPs who are well-informed on a particular subject. Overall, Select Committees have helped contribute to an improvement in the quality of debate. The House has an opportunity at report stage to discuss important changes made to a Bill in committee. Important points fed in at committee stage by affected groups are likely to be rehearsed again at this stage. Even without attempting to have any direct influence on proceedings on the Floor of the House groups can none the less – through their activity on the committee corridor of the Palace of Westminster – have some input into the deliberations taking place in the chamber.

Direct influence on deliberation in the chamber is diverse and not easily quantifiable. MPs have to declare any relevant pecuniary interests when contributing to debate[40] but, where no such interest exists, they do not have to indicate the genesis of a particular idea or amendment they are putting forward; indeed, they may themselves not know its origins: an idea may have been fed to them by a group via another MP, or a constituent, or a newspaper story, or an MP's research assistant. Nor is it possible to prove a causal relationship between lobbying and an MP's parliamentary behaviour. The fact that an MP is lobbied by, say, the Police Federation and subsequently praises the police in a debate on the subject does not prove that such lobbying has proved influential; the MP may have intended all along to praise the police.

However, sufficient evidence exists to advance two generalisations. One is that MPs (and peers) are now the object of considerable lobbying by outside groups. As we have recorded already, the 1986 survey of sectional and promotional groups found that a majority maintained regular contact with one or more MPs. Of those maintaining such contact, one in three regularly or often sent material or briefings to all or a large number of MPs. More than 80 per cent had asked an MP to table a motion.[41] The second generalisation is that, despite this increase, the opportunities for pursuing the points raised by outside groups are limited. For groups pursuing a proactive stance the limitations are severe. The timetable of the House of Commons is determined principally by government. The opportunities for backbench MPs to raise issues on their own initiative are few, comprising essentially Question Time, the half-hour adjournment debate at the end of the day, and Private Members' Time. The daily adjournment debate is used most often to raise issues of non-partisan concern (for example, the problem of solvent abuse) and constituency issues on which the Member seeks a more substantial response than is possible at Question Time. Question Time is becoming increasingly crowded by questions tabled by Opposition MPs to make partisan points and, in response, questions tabled by government backbenchers designed to allow ministers to make positive comments on government activity. Questions prompted by pressure groups are more likely to take the form of written questions and, as such, do not form part of parliamentary debate; they are, though, the subject of increasing criticism because of the amount of civil service time now taken up in answering them. Private Members' Time is a focus for pressure group activity, but this was so before the 1970s: pressure groups lobby MPs to introduce Private Members' Bills. However, such is the demand that selection is by ballot: in each session the first six MPs whose names are drawn in the ballot will have their Bills debated. Once the names of the six are known they become the target of frenetic lobbying. However, the proportion of Private Members' Bills originating from pressure groups is not increasing. Rather the reverse: MPs are increasingly likely to choose measures suggested by government departments, knowing that they have a much greater chance of getting them passed.[42] On the basis of this evidence, there is little to suggest that groups seeking to fulfil an agenda-setting role have much greater success now than they did twenty years or more ago.

Groups adopting a reactive stance have much greater opportunities to influence proceedings. Government sets the agenda but groups are now much more active in seeking to influence the items on that agenda. The most spectacular example of such influence has already been identified: the defeat of the Shops Bill on Second Reading. Of groups in the 1986 survey who had been concerned by recent legislation before the House, just over half (53 per cent) had asked MPs to speak during the Second Reading debate. Though such input is not going to affect the outcome of the vote – with the one notable exception of the Shops Bill – it is useful in signalling the group's position and may have some impact on the government's stance at committee or report stage. Persuading an MP to put one's case at Second Reading may be helpful in another respect: speaking at Second Reading increases the chances of a Member being selected to serve on the Standing Committee.

Group lobbying also takes place on topical issues debated by the House. Affected groups will lobby MPs, either by mail or in person: early in 1990, for example, during an industrial dispute involving members of the ambulance service, ambulance drivers were to be seen lobbying not only Opposition MPs but also Conservative backbenchers; some sympathetic Conservative MPs then volunteered to act as go-betweens in the dispute. Mass lobbies of Parliament, with members of a particular pressure group crowding the Central Lobby or the Grand Committee Room, are regular features of parliamentary life. Such lobbying will sometimes have a permeating effect, entering the consciousness of MPs and thereby having some potential for being raised in the chamber – though whether the potential is realised depends upon the business of the House (predominantly government-determined) and catching the Speaker's eye. The greater the number of sympathetic MPs, the greater the likelihood of a group's case being advanced.

Lobbying by groups adds to the strain on the resources of the Palace of Westminster and the same argument concerning the divide between well-resourced and less-well-resourced groups continues in the context of such lobbying. However, many of the mass lobbies are conducted by group activists rather than professional lobbyists and though not the most efficient form of lobbying, provides an opportunity for any group with committed activists to get its view over to Members of Parliament. Overall, direct lobbying – by ensuring that parliamentarians are aware of the views and concerns of different groups in society – contributes to a better-informed House. The pressure on resources remains a problem; but, as various commentators have suggested, that should prompt an expansion of resources rather than a restriction on the existing opportunities to lobby Members. The disparity in access to Parliament remains, but that suggests the need for a wider education of groups as to the channels available for making representations, rather than limiting those who already enjoy such access. The discussion takes place in the context of a continuing growth in parliamentary lobbying. Lobbyists, and more especially lobbying, are not going away.

THE 'AMERICANISATION' OF BRITISH POLITICS?

The growth in lobbying, and especially the emergence of professional lobbyists, invites obvious comparison with the position in the United States. Many of the practices employed in the United States are now found in the United Kingdom. The emergence of firms of political consultants – some with links with lobbying firms on Capitol Hill – and the techniques they employ (wining and dining MPs and peers, arranging private meetings with ministers and civil servants) has led a number of commentators to believe, or rather fear, the 'Americanisation' of British politics. The perception is a plausible one. However, it is difficult to sustain.

There is little evidence of a conscious emulation of American practice. The explanations offered for the growth of lobbying are essentially indigenous to Britain. Furthermore, and more importantly, lobbying – especially professional lobbying – remains limited, both in extent and effect. By comparison with US experience, professional lobbying in Britain is small business; the annual turnover of British consultancy firms in total is probably not much more than £10 million,[43] less than the turnover of some individual public-relations firms. Though there is scope for the expansion of lobbying activities it is not likely to approach the level of lobbying in the USA; and it is constrained from ever having the same impact. The reason for this is to be found in political parties and the ideological environment in which they are nurtured. Operating within a broad ideological consensus political parties in the USA are weak entities, both in terms of policy generation and mobilising electoral support. Candidates are heavily dependent upon personal resources or the resources offered by groups, especially those channelled now through Political Action Committees. Parties do not provide a protective cloak against the pressures of well-organised groups. There is some evidence that various members of the House and Senate have failed to gain re-election as a result of negative campaigning by groups opposed to their candidature: Birch Bayh in Iowa, for example, and Joseph Tydings in Maryland.

In Britain, by contrast, there is no ideological consensus. There is an ideological divide between right and left and, despite some evidence of partisan de-alignment in the 1970s and 1980s, there is still strong attachment to party. Election campaigns – at national and now at local level – are fought on party lines; with few exceptions the party label determines the outcome. Party provides the campaign resources for candidates: party activists carry out the mundane tasks of addressing envelopes and doorstep canvassing; the party provides the campaign funding, operating within statutory – and enforced – limits. Individual candidates do not have to raise their own resources: their dependence is on party and not on outside benefactors. Party thus provides their essential point of reference. It also provides a shield against assault by pressure groups. MPs find the activities of such groups useful in providing them with information and advice and such lobbying has helped give them a new lease of life. However, where a clash arises between party and pressure group, the party is normally assured of victory. Party provides the basic context for parliamentary deliberations, especially on the Floor of the House; though no longer guaranteeing the outcome of votes on every occasion, it continues to determine the outcome on virtually every occasion. Party thus provides a clear delimiting framework within which lobbying takes place, a framework that is largely absent in the United States. British experience is now closer to that of the United States but the gap remains a wide one.

CONCLUSION

The past two decades have witnessed a significant increase in parliamentary lobbying, by both pressure groups and constituents, in Britain. By American standards the activity is modest. By British standards it is extensive. It has placed strains on parliamentary resources. It has generated debate, and official concern, about uneven access to the Palace of Westminster. However, the effect on parliamentary deliberations has been a beneficial one for Parliament. It has helped provide Members of Parliament with more information and with alternative sources of advice to that offered by government. It has provided for better-informed Standing and Select Committees. The consequence has been a Parliament better equipped to subject government to scrutiny and influence. Parliament is now a more effective policy-influencing legislature than at any previous time in the twentieth century. Party remains the basic determinant of parliamentary behaviour and the strength of party stands as a bar to Parliament ever regaining the characteristics of a policy-making assembly. However, the activities of pressure groups and of constituents has helped reduce the rough edges of partisan conflict and afforded Parliament a more significant role in the political system. The more that role is recognised, the greater the strength of Parliament.

NOTES

1. A. B. White, *The Making of the English Constitution, 449–1485* (New York: G. P. Putnam's Sons, 1908) Part III, ch. 3.
2. M. Mezey, *Comparative Legislatures* (Durham, N. C.: Duke University Press, 1979); P. Norton, 'Parliament and Policy in Britain: the House of Commons as a Policy Influencer', *Teaching Politics*, 13 (2), May 1984, pp. 198–221.

3. See J. B. Conacher (ed.), *The Emergence of British Parliamentary Democracy in the Nineteenth Century* (New York: Wiley, 1971).

4. A. L. Lowell, *The Government of England*, vol. 2 (New York: Macmillan, 1924) pp. 74–81.

5. S. H. Beer, *Modern British Politics* (London: Faber, 1969) p. 350.

6. Before 1950 it was possible for Conservative candidates to contribute substantial sums to their local parties and, in effect, purchase their candidatures; the practice was ended following the Maxwell-Fyfe Report of 1948.

7. I. Gilmour, *The Body Politic*, rev. edn (London: Hutchinson, 1971) p. 261.

8. R. Klein, 'Policy Making in the National Health Service', *Political Studies*, 22 (1), 1974, p. 6.

9. A. G. Jordan and J. J. Richardson, 'The British Policy Style or the Logic of Neogotiation?', in J. J. Richardson (ed.), *Policy Styles in Western Europe* (London: George Allen & Unwin, 1982).

10. This was especially so in the latter half of the 1960s when several major measures of social reform – on divorce, abortion and homosexuality – were enacted through the medium of Private Members' legislation. See P. G. Richards, *Parliament and Conscience* (London: George Allen & Unwin, 1970).

11. See, for details of activity early in the decade, R. E. Dowse, 'The MP and His Surgery', *Political Studies*, 11, 1963, pp. 333–41.

12. See J. Marsh, 'The House of Commons: Representational Changes', in P. Norton (ed.), *Parliament in the 1980s* (Oxford: Basil Blackwell, 1985) p. 69.

13. The 1990 edition of *Dod's Parliamentary Companion* lists 35 such firms. For a substantial discussion on the number and nature of political consultancy firms, see C. Grantham and C. Seymour-Ure, 'Parliament and Political Consultants', in M. Rush (ed.), *Parliament and Pressure Politics* (Oxford: Oxford University Press, 1990).

14. C. Grantham, 'Parliament and Political Consultants', *Parliamentary Affairs*, 42 (4), 1989, p. 505.

15. *The Financial Times*, 23 December 1985.

16. The data are contained in Rush (ed.), *Parliament and Pressure Politics*.

17. A survey by the Letter Writing Bureau in 1986 found that a Member would on average receive between 20 and 50 letters a day. J. A. G. Griffith and M. Ryle, *Parliament: Functions, Practice and Procedures* (London: Sweet & Maxwell, 1989) p. 72.

18. The 1971 survey of MPs by the Review Body on Top Salaries found that backbenchers spent approximately 11 hours a week outside the House working on constituency business; the 1982 survey found that the average had increased to 16 hours. A 1984 survey by the Commons Reform Group found that a majority of respondents spent eight or more days a month in the constituency when the House was sitting; one in five spent 13 or more days a month in the constituency.

19. The figures are aggregated from a series of parliamentary answers given by ministers in response to questions tabled by Austin Mitchell MP in 1982 and James Cran MP in 1989.

20. See P. Regan, 'The 1986 Shops Bill', *Parliamentary Affairs*, 41 (2), 1988, pp. 218–35.

21. See Grantham and Seymour-Ure, 'Parliament and Political Consultants'.

22. P. Shipley, *Directory of Pressure Groups and Representative Organisations*, 2nd edn (London: Bowker, 1979).

23. See Grantham, 'Parliament and Political Consultants', p. 508.

24. See P. Norton, *Dissension in the House of Commons, 1945–74* (London: Macmillan, 1974); P. Norton, *Conservative Dissidents* (London: Temple Smith, 1978).

25.   P. Norton, *Dissension in the House of Commons, 1974–79* (Oxford: Oxford University Press, 1980) pp. 491–3.

26.   P. Norton, 'The House of Commons: Behavioural Changes', in Norton (ed.), *Parliament in the 1980s*, pp. 22–47.

27,   The Select Committee on Scottish Affairs was not reappointed in the 1987 Parliament because of difficulties encountered in getting Scottish Conservative MPs to serve on it.

28.   See C. Mellors, *The British MP* (Farnborough: Saxon House, 1978), and A. King, 'The Rise of the Career Politician in Britain – and its Consequences', *British Journal of Political Science*, 2 (3), 1981, pp. 249–85.

29.   See P. Norton and D. Wood, 'Constituency Service by British MPs – Does it Contribute to a Personal Vote?', *Parliamentary Affairs*, 43 (2), April 1990, pp. 196–208.

30.   See P. Norton, *Memorandum of Evidence* submitted to the Select Committee on Procedure, Session 1989–90.

31.   See especially the Second Report from the Select Committee on Procedure, Session 1984–85: *Public Bill Procedure* HC 49 (London: Her Majesty's Stationery Office, 1985). In 1986 the House failed to approve the most radical of the Committee's recommendations, that of automatic timetabling of Bills.

32.   See J. E. Schwarz, 'Exploring a New Role in Policy Making: the British House of Commons in the 1970s', *American Political Science Review*, 74 (1), 1980, pp. 23–37.

33.   P. Norton, 'Public Legislation', in Rush (ed.), *Parliament and Pressure Politics*.

34.   Ibid.

35.   Labour MP to author.

36.   Norton, 'Public Legislation'.

37.   Ibid.

38.   C. Grantham and C. M. Hodgson, 'The House of Lords: Structural Changes', in Norton (ed.), *Parliament in the 1980s*, p. 115.

39.   The effect of Committees on policy is difficult to assess in quantitative terms. However, in a parliamentary answer in 1986 the Prime Minister listed those recommendations made by Select Committees in the year from March 1985 to March 1986 which the government had accepted: in sum, 150 recommendations were listed.

40.   Failure to do so is considered a serious offence. In February 1990 the House voted to suspend for one month the Conservative MP for Winchester for failing to declare his interests when raising certain matters on the Floor of the House. Shortly afterwards the MP announced that he would not be seeking re-election at the next General Election.

41.   Rush (ed.), *Parliament and Pressure Politics*.

42.   D. Marsh and M. Read, *Private Members' Bills* (Cambridge: Cambridge University Press, 1988).

43.   Grantham, 'Parliament and Political Consultants', p. 505.

5. Now Nobody Understands the System: The Changing Face of Local Government*

R. A. W. Rhodes

When Michael Heseltine became Secretary of State for the Environment in 1979 he was amazed at the complexities of local government finance. He defended his massive Local Government, Planning and Land Bill on the grounds that the existing system was so arcane that only three people in the country understood it. When he left the Department for the Ministry of Defence in 1983 he had an enviable achievement to his credit – nobody understood the system. Little has changed in the intervening years.

During the 1980s some 40 Acts affecting local government were passed.[1] The scale of the activity was daunting and its consequences were both manifold and unintended. This chapter provides a survey of developments and seeks to answer the question, 'What has changed, by how much and why?'

For many commentators there might seem to be an obvious answer to the question: the 1980s witnessed the demise of local government and an unprecedented degree of centralisation. Indeed, as early as 1980 commentators had begun to decry Whitehall's 'takeover' of local government.[2] Somewhat surprisingly, commentators are still talking about a 'revolution in local government' and a 'radical change'.[3] Presumably, therefore, the intervening years witnessed something less than a revolution. Local government's demise has been delayed by some ten years. This chapter explores the paradox of the alleged demise of local government in 1980 and the projected comprehensive reform after 1987, arguing that the centre's relations with local government have been characterised more by unintended consequences than by a revolution. Centralisation there may have been, but the most important consequence of central policy towards local government in the 1980s is that it has generated a *policy mess*[4] in which neither level of government can achieve its objectives.

Three final points by way of introduction. First, I have drawn on my earlier work in preparing this chapter.[5] Secondly, many accounts of local government discuss the likely effects of legislation: all too frequently they are prognostications of doom. Evaluations based on the actual effects of government policy are less common. For the period 1979–87 I focus on the actual effects of government policy. Thereafter my comments are more speculative but continue to be informed by the view that what the government wants it frequently does not get. Finally, the narrative is structured around the three Parliaments of the 1980s. Such divisions are not a matter of convenience or idleness. Each General Election marks an intensification of government policy towards local government.

The remainder of the chapter falls into two sections. First, I explore the major trends in government policy between 1979–83, 1983–7 and post-1987. Secondly, I offer an overall assessment of the period, an explanation of the twists and turns of events, and a review of the possible futures facing local government in the 1990s.

TRENDS IN INTERGOVERNMENTAL RELATIONS

In spite of rumours to the contrary, Britain was not created afresh in 1979. The relations between Westminster, Whitehall and the rest of the government machine – referred to collectively as intergovernmental relations (IGR) – have deep historical roots. Without going into detail, several features of IGR in the postwar period have conditioned policy in the 1980s.

First, British central government is 'non-executant': that is, central departments do not directly deliver services to citizens. Apart from the obvious exceptions of defence and social security, major services such as housing, education, health and personal social services are provided by, for example, local authorities. As a result, although it passes the laws and provides a substantial proportion of the finance, the centre is dependent upon other bodies for the success of policies which can greatly affect the government's electoral fortunes.

Secondly, local authorities played a key role in the development of the welfare state. The growth in their financial resources did not, however, keep pace with the growth in their responsibilities. Expansion was paid for by the centre. With economic recession and the drive to restrain public expenditure, local government was a prime target for cuts.

Thirdly, cuts in public expenditure in general and local expenditure in particular are not peculiar to Conservative governments. Spurred on by the oil crisis and the terms of the IMF loan, Labour governments of the 1970s sought to restrain local expenditure and deployed monetarist economic means to that end. In other words, national economic management problems have a pervasive influence on IGR.

Fourthly, the administrative structure of Britain is not unitary but differentiated. Not only are there distinct administrative systems in Scotland, Wales and Northern Ireland but there is also a range of public-sector organisations including nationalised industries and non-departmental public bodies (sometimes referred to as Quangos) as well as local authorities. Whilst the latter may be the pre-eminent institution beyond Whitehall, obviously such bodies as regional and district health authorities are important in terms of both expenditure and relevance to citizens. Moreover, this diversity of institutions is matched by the diversity of interests within the centre between, for example, the Treasury guarding the public purse and the spending departments.

Fifthly, although the centre needs local authorities to deliver services and local authorities need the centre to provide the money and the authority for their actions, this interdependence is not between equals. The relationship is asymmetric: the centre can unilaterally pass an Act changing the relationship. There is a recurrent tension between this capacity for authoritative decision-making by central government and the interdependence of centre and locality.

Finally, Britain is a 'dual polity'[6] wherein national and local political élites are insulated from each other and the centre distances itself from local affairs. In sharp contrast to the French system Britain has neither a Napoleonic tradition of using central field agents (or prefects) to supervise local authorities nor a system of *cumul des mandats* whereby politicians accumulate electoral offices leading to the close interpenetration of national and local élites. The British territorial operating code stresses the autonomy of the centre in matters of high politics.

All of these factors have been constant features of IGR in Britain in the postwar period, conditioning the practice of Conservative and Labour governments. A focus on specific pieces of legislation can prove seriously misleading. Any adequate analysis of IGR has to cover the range of public-sector organisations and the context within which they operate. This account of the 1980s is no exception.[7]

1979–83: REPRISE

Like Max Bygraves this section could tell a story. There is some merit in the approach. Mrs Thatcher's governments succeeded in doing the unthinkable. They rescued students from the terminal boredom of lectures on local government by making the subject interesting, even humorous for those with a taste for black comedy. Unfortunately, space precludes such a relaxed expansive narrative. I will restrict myself to a brief description of the distinctive features of the period, namely: intervention and control, unilateralism, litigation, risk avoidance, recalcitrance, and unintended consequences.

Intervention and control

The 'problem' of local government finance is not new, although definitions of the problem and the choice of solution vary greatly.[8] There are some constants. Central government's concern is marked less by the search for a sound system of local government finance than by its preoccupation with national economic management problems. The 1979 Conservative government committed itself not only to reducing public expenditure but also to riding out a world economic recession. Local authorities were expected to bear the brunt of the cuts.

The means for attaining the 'cuts' were provided by the Local Government, Planning and Land Act 1980 which introduced grant penalties. In effect, any local authority spending more than the government's estimate of what it needed to spend would lose central government grant at an increasing rate. The government also reduced the total amount of grant to local authorities from 61 per cent to 53 per cent of their expenditure and imposed tight ceilings on capital expenditure. The response of local authorities was to increase the rates or local property tax to compensate for this loss of grant. Local authority current expenditure – for example, expenditure on salaries, lighting, heating – continued to rise in real terms – that is, disregarding wage increases and inflation. By 1983 it was 9 per cent higher than in 1979. On the other hand, capital expenditure – such as expenditure on fixed assets like buildings – fell by 12 per cent over the same period and the total number of local government employees fell by some 4 per cent. At best, the Conservatives record of success can be described as mixed.[9]

A government committed to pushing back the frontiers of the state intervened massively in local affairs. Distinctively, it sought direct control of total local expenditure (not just central grant) of each individual local authority; especially high-spending Labour councils. The policy may not have been successful but the search for control was on and the search was not restricted to local finance: for example, the sale of council houses was imposed upon local authorities.

Unilateralism

The Government's style paralleled its policies. When confronted by the need to cut public expenditure the previous Labour government had set up the Consultative Council on Local Government Finance (CCLGF) as a vehicle for negotiating with, and eliciting the co-operation of, local authorities. Michael Heseltine was not so inclined and the Conservative government as a whole had little faith in consultation, or in any device which smacked of 'corporatism'. The CCLGF became 'a forum where they start telling you what you're going to do'. Consultation was abandoned. Michael Heseltine used the CCLGF to announce what he was going to do, usually after he had briefed the press. This shift epitomises the government's style: it knew best and consequently saw no need to consult and negotiate. Unilateralism was the order of the day.[11]

Litigation

The response of local authorities to the government's unilateral style was to look for ways of getting around the legislation. The legal profession was an unexpected beneficiary of government policy as litigious behaviour and the search for judge-proof legislation came to mark IGR. Indeed, these trends are a clear indicator of the breakdown in 'normal processes'. Nor was the conflict restricted to central government and local authorities (as in the clash between Norwich and the Secretary of State for the Environment over the sale of council houses): it extended to conflicts between Labour and Conservative local authorities (as in the clash between Bromley London Borough and the Greater London Council over subsidies to the London Transport Executive).[12]

Risk Avoidance

The Local Government, Planning and Land Act 1980 was certainly compendious but it was not definitive. Between 1979 and 1983 there were seven major changes to the grant system.[13] The immediate consequence of so many changes was instability. Local authorities were given various and incompatible spending targets. Even local authorities which supported the government budgeted to minimise the effect of the changes. Their risk avoidance strategies took a number of forms. For example, local authorities were reluctant to incur capital expenditure because of the knock-on effect on current expenditure. Creative accountancy flourished. Expenditures were reclassified. Statistics were massaged. Rates were increased, not to cover committed expenditure, but to build up reserves as a precaution against future changes. The cast of mind in local government is amply illustrated by this reaction of an official: 'We've always taken government targets seriously until we got this 5.6 per cent reduction (1981–2) which we didn't take seriously because we don't think anyone could seriously mean it.'[14]

In effect local government did not know what money it had to spend and the centre did not know what local authorities would spend.

Recalcitrance

As the government abandoned consultation for unilateralism, so local authorities abandoned co-operation for confrontation. Thus, Labour-controlled local authorities continued to increase their expenditure and to exceed their spending targets. The Greater London Council (GLC) and Inner London Education Authority (ILEA) both exceeded their spending targets to such an extent that they received no central grant. Full-blooded confrontation took place over subsidies for public transport. For example, Labour introduced a 25 per cent reduction in bus and tube fares in London which led to a large increase in the GLC's expenditure. This 'Fares Fair' policy not only upset the Conservative government but also the Conservative-controlled London boroughs. Bromley council successfully challenged the policy in the courts but 18 months later Labour had a revamped policy in place and the government introduced the Transport Act (1982) giving itself the power to limit transport subsidies. For both the GLC and the metropolitan county councils (MCCs) transport subsidies were a major factor in their 'overspending', a deliberate and conspicuous challenge to government policy.

Unintended Consequences

'Cuts' in local expenditure proved elusive. The record for individual programmes was mixed. Housing expenditure fell by some 49 per cent, law and order expenditure rose by 19 per cent and defence expenditure by 14 per cent, all in line with government priorities. But expenditure on education remained constant in real terms. Health expenditure rose by some 6 per cent and social security expenditure rose by some 25 per cent, not at all in line with government priorities. Whatever else the Conservative government may have intended, a continuing increase in real terms in public expenditure in general and local current expenditure in particular was *not* an objective.

The continuous changes to the grant system are the major unintended consequence of Conservative policy on local government finance, reflecting the failure of expenditure policy. There are other examples. Thus the expenditure squeeze has impeded the transfer of patients from the NHS to 'care in the community' by local authorities.[15] Similarly, local authorities were forced to increase council house rents. Around half of these increases were paid by the Department of Health and Social Security (DHSS) because tenants were unemployed or pensioners or on supplementary benefit.

The Conservatives' first Parliament ended, therefore, with its policy towards local government in a state of some disrepair. Repeated exhortations, repeated legislation, repeated changes to the grant system produced the same outcome: growth in local current expenditure. Ever pragmatists, the Conservatives entered the 1983 election urging councils to spend more on capital projects such as the modernisation of old housing stock. The lesson of 1979–83 seemed clear. Commands, formal powers of control and bureaucratic intervention were a poor substitute for a system based on voluntary co-operation. It is tempting to conclude that the harder successive Secretaries of State tried, the more they got – of what they didn't want! The government drew a different conclusion; if thwarted, then retaliate.

1983–7: RETALIATION

The government's policy on local government during their second term originated in a Cabinet sub-committee chaired by William Whitelaw, the Treasury's wish for direct controls over local expenditure, and Mrs Thatcher's determination to 'do something' about local government.[16] Abolition of the GLC and the MCCs and rate-capping became official policy. Once again, in the interests of economy, I focus on the distinctive features of the period: namely, abolition, 'cuts', repetitive legislation, politicisation, instability, and differentiation.

Abolition

As a general rule the Conservative government of the 1980s avoided structural reform. The policy towards local government after 1983 was one exception. The government abolished the GLC and the MCCs. It also created a range of *ad hoc* bodies to replace these councils and to bypass local authorities (see below). In effect, if local government would not do as it was told, it would be replaced or ignored.

The stated objective of abolition was to:

> streamline local government in the metropolitan areas. It will remove a source of conflict and tension. It will save money, after some transitional costs. It will also provide a system which is simpler for the public to understand, in that responsibility for virtually all services will rest with a single authority.[17]

Norman Tebbitt offered a blunter assessment. The GLC was abolished because it was Labour dominated, high-spending and at odds with the government's view of the world.[18] There were numerous political miscalculations in the process of abolition. It ate up a massive amount of parliamentary time. Yet Mrs Thatcher was able to work another of her minor miracles. Ken Livingstone (Labour Group leader on the GLC) was transformed from a political pariah – the friend of the IRA, gays and any other group the tabloids profit from deriding – into a charming, articulate television personality. Truly, butter would not melt in his mouth. This transformation also illustrates an important feature of the abolition of the GLC and the MCCs. Any attempted explanation must beware of adopting an overly rationalist approach. Above all the policy was a 'Nietzschean folly' – 'theatrical', 'dramatic' and 'a British farce'.[19]

What replaced the GLC and the MCCs? The question admits of no easy answer. The position for the MCCs is summarised in Table 5.1. Quite clearly the new system is complex and it is no simpler in London. More important than the number of agencies is the fact that a significant proportion of them are not directly or even indirectly elected. For example, only 33 per cent of the expenditure on local services in London is by the directly elected boroughs. The remaining expenditure is by central departments, quangos, private companies, London-wide indirectly elected bodies and part-London indirectly elected bodies.[20]

What were the consequences of these changes? In 1939 William Robson described the government of London as a 'chaos of areas and authorities'.[21] London is again misgoverned with its ambiguous and complex distribution of functions and institutions. Fragmentation and the erosion of local political control characterise its government. Equivalent problems beset the metropolitan areas. In addition, there are the problems originating in the muddle of the middle tier. The indirectly elected bodies are under mixed political control and lack political leadership. The re-allocation of functions has fuelled inter-borough and inter-district conflict and yet there is no mechanism for resolving it. Joint committees lack consensus and are slow to respond to new problems. The constituent boroughs of joint boards and joint commitees tend to be parochial, complacent and to manifest a narrowness of purpose.[22] Returning to the government's stated objectives, conflict has intensified, the system has not been simplified and responsibility does not rest with a single authority. Moreover, although there has been no official analysis of the savings, Skelcher and Leach estimate that expenditure *rose* by 4 per cent between 1984–5 and 1987–8 on the services transferred from the MCCs to the districts.[23]

There is one final consequence: the reformed structure is unstable. Since the Local Government Act (1985) the government has abolished the Inner London Education Authority (ILEA) and the Labour Party proposes to introduce regional government. The future remains unstable. Only one thing is clear:

> The future design of London government will be neither the product of administrative rationality or academic reflection, nor the by-product of allegedly inexorable economic or social processes. Rather it will be shaped largely as a product of party political interests, political ideologies, party conflicts and coalitions.[24]

'Cuts'

By abolishing the GLC and the MCCs the government removed seven 'over-spending' councils. The policy was one of two prongs designed to cut local expenditure. The second prong was rate-capping. The Rates Act 1984 gave the Secretary of State for the Environment power to determine an 'over-spending' council's maximum rate. The total number of local

Table 5.1:   *Post-abolition arrangements in the six Metropolitan County Council areas*

		Greater Manchester	Merseyside	South Yorkshire
A.	**Scope of county-wide voluntary joint arrangements**			
	Waste regulation & disposal	Statutory jt board 0 imposed by Minister (excl. Wigan for waste disposal – permitted to secede)	Statutory jt board 0 imposed by Minister	Indiv. MDCs + 1 purely advisory jt c'ttee; central hazardous waste unit
	Trading standards/ consumer protection	Indiv. MDCs + jt 2 c'ttee; county-wide scientific services unit	Indiv. MDCs + jt 1 c'ttee	Indiv. MDCs + jt 1 c'ttee; small county-wide unit
	Planning	R & I unit + 4 several specialist units: Countryside Unit, Minerals & Waste Disposal Unit; Tree Bank	R & I unit 4 combined with transportation modelling unit; 3-district Countryside Advisory Service; urban traffic control scheme	Minimal; small 1 mining advisory unit
	Highways and traffic	Transportation 3 modelling unit; 3-district highways consortium; jt urban traffic control scheme, etc.		Minimal 0
	Section 48 collective funding scheme for grants to voluntary organisations	Large scheme; jt 5 grants c'ttee serviced by AGMA; Grants Unit	No s.48 scheme 0	No s.48 scheme 0
	Other services	County Records 1 Office + Archaeo-logical Unit retained (no jt c'ttee)	Minimal 0	Minimal 0
	(Overall score)	(15)	(5)	(3)

	Tyne & Wear	West Midlands	West Yorkshire
A. Scope of county-wide Voluntary joint arrangements			
Waste regulation & disposal	Indiv. MDCs + jt c'ttee with some delegated powers; central hazardous waste unit 2	Indiv. MDCs + jt c'ttee with some delegated powers; co-ordination unit respons. for strategic plg + hazardous waste monitoring 2	Jt c'ttee respons. for discharging all waste management functions; county-wide service retained intact 5
Trading standards/ consumer protection	Indiv. MDCs + jt c'ttee; joint arrangements for certain functions 1	Indiv. MDCs + jt c'ttee; small central unit 1	Jt c'ttee, with county service retained largely intact 5
Planning	R & I unit combined with transportation modelling unit; urban traffic control scheme; misc. county-wide highways functions (e.g. accident records, Tyne Bridges) 5	R & I unit combined with transportation modelling unit 3	Minimal (discontinued R & I unit) 0
Highways and traffic			County-wide Highways, Engineering & Transportation Services (HETS) 5
Section 48 collective funding scheme for grants to voluntary organisations	Intermediate but declining scheme; co-ordinating c'ttee 2	Small scheme; jt c'ttee 2	Intermediate scheme; grants jt c'ttee, serviced by Grants Unit 3
Other services	Archaeology & Building Preservation team retained; county-wide archives service supervised by jt c'ttee 3	Minimal 0	Archives & Archaeology service retained, under supervision of jt c'ttee 2
(Overall score)	(13)	(8)	(20)

Table 5.1 continued

		Greater Manchester	Merseyside	South Yorkshire
B.	**Degree of commitment to county-wide joint arrangements**			
	Scope of county-wide voluntary joint arrangements (from Section A above)	Extensive	Limited	Negligible
	Stability of jt. arrangements	Moderate	Moderate	Moderate
	Influence of co-ordinating committee and/or other co-ordinating arrangements	Considerable	Negligible	Strong
C.	**Operational style of joint arrangements**			
	Predominant style of co-ordinating arrangements	Formal	Formal	Mixed
	Form of servicing of joint boards and committees	Lead Authority	Lead Authority	Central servicing unit – S. Yorks Jt Secretariat
	Joint board chair/ lead authority link	No	Yes, but breaking down	Not applicable
	Police Joint Board	Lead – Salford Chair – Wigan	Lead – Knowsley Chair – Knowsley	Chair – Rotherham
	Fire & Civil Defence Board	Lead – Wigan Chair – Stockport	Lead – Liverpool Chair – Wirral	Chair – Barnsley
	Passenger Transport Board	Lead – Manchester Chair – Bolton	Lead – part PTA – Mersey Travel Chair – St Helens	Chair – Doncaster
	Waste Disposal Board	Lead – Oldham Chair – Tameside	Lead – St Helens Chair – St Helens	Not applicable
	Pensions Board	Not applicable	Not applicable	Chair – Sheffield (since 1988)

Reproduced, with permission, from S. Leach and H. Davies, 'Introduction', *Local Government Studies*, 16, 1990, p. 3. My thanks to Chris Game (INLOGOV, University of Birmingham) for supplying this amended version.

	Tyne & Wear	West Midlands	West Yorkshire
B. Degree of commitment to county-wide joint arrangements			
Scope of county-wide voluntary joint arrangements (from Section A above)	Moderate	Limited	Extensive
Stability of jt. arrangements	High	Moderate	High, after early fragility
Influence of co-ordinating committee and/or other co-ordinating arrangements	Moderate	Moderate	Considerable, but informal
C. Operational style of joint arrangements			
Predominant style of co-ordinating arrangements	Formal	Formal	Informal
Form of servicing of joint boards and committees	Lead Authority	Lead Authority	Lead Authority
Joint board chair/ lead authority link	Yes	Yes, but breaking down	Yes
Police Joint Board	Lead – Gateshead Chair – Gateshead	Lead – Dudley Chair – Dudley	Lead – Wakefield Chair – Wakefield
Fire & Civil Defence Board	Lead – Sunderland Chair – Sunderland	Lead – Sandwell Chair – Sandwell	Lead – part Kirklees part FCDA Chair – Kirklees
Passenger Transport Board	Lead – Newcastle Chair – Newcastle	Lead – Coventry Chair – Wolverhampton	Lead – part Leeds part PTA Chair – Leeds
Waste Disposal Board	Not applicable	Not applicable	Not applicable
Pensions Board	Not applicable	Not applicable	Not applicable

authorities capped has been small and the policy made only a marginal contribution to slowing down the rate of increase in local current expenditure. Between 1983–4 and 1987–8 local current expenditure rose by 11 per cent in real terms whilst capital expenditure, after rising by some 19 per cent at the time of the 1983 General Election, continued its downward trend. The total number of local government employees rose. The government itself conceded that local current expenditure had risen by 1.5 per cent per annum in real terms in the 1980s.

The proportion of local expenditure funded by central grant continued to fall (to 46 per cent in 1987). Distinctively, an age-old means of central control returned to favour: the specific grant. Such grants now account for approximately a quarter of total grant to local authorities. But overall local authority expenditure continued to increase in real terms.

The response of the government was *Paying for Local Government*,[25] which heralded the community charge, better known as poll tax. It was not the only significant proposal (see below) but the immediate impact of the Green Paper was muted. The government was waiting for a third term of office before resuming its attack on the 'problem' of local government. There was a stand-off. Grant settlements were more favourable to local government. Volume targets were abolished. The increase in local expenditure continued. 'You can't throw money at problems, money isn't the answer. ... But there was one exception to the rule. You could throw money at a General Election.'[26] The brakes were off. More important, the radical government had lost its sense of direction. The local government stand-off is one instance of this drift in government policy and, perhaps, it epitomises the government's second term of office.[27] It was the lull before the storm.

Repetitive legislation

The spate of legislation may not have had the desired effects but the quantity of legislation is also revealing. Aaron Wildavsky has described the process of repetitive budgeting wherein budgets are made and remade throughout the year because of the high degree of uncertainty surrounding income.[28] By analogy, repetitive legislation is the process wherein laws are made and remade throughout a term of office because of the high degree of uncertainty surrounding its viability. The sheer volume of local government legislation in the 1980s, especially on local government finance, is evidence of this process. Legislation was enacted, found wanting either in the courts or in its desired impact thereby prompting a new bill ostensibly to remedy the defects but in fact to create yet more defects and consequent legislative activity.

Instability and more

Instability continued and was intensified by both repetitive legislation and the complexity of the fragmented governmental structures of the conurbations, the growing number of non-departmental public bodies (see below) and separate policies in Scotland and Northern Ireland.[29] Both the Audit Commission and the Comptroller and Auditor General concluded that the grant system was causing inefficiency and ineffectiveness in local government. The former pointed to the unnecessary accumulation of some £1200 million in reserves to counter uncertainty.[30] Clarity was scarcely helped by the transitional funding arrangements surrounding the abolition of the GLC and the MCCs.

To compound the effects of instability and complexity the grant system was also generating inequitable and arbitrary outcomes. Moderate, cost conscious Conservative-controlled councils found themselves subject to grant penalties. Urban authorities facing major social and economic problems were starved of funds. Local authorities which participated in youth employment programmes found that funds from the Manpower Services Commission (MSC) served to increase the grant penalties imposed by government. Some of the effects were deliberate; the government redistributed grant in favour of the county councils. Other effects were unintended; the various grant formulae used population growth as an indicator of need thereby diverting grant from declining urban areas. It would seem that stability had become anathema and that the system was generating perverse outcomes.

Politicisation

Local authorities remained willing to challenge the government in the courts but their main response to the waves of legislation was political. The GLC and the MCCs mounted a professional public relations campaign against abolition. Liverpool council drew the Secretary of State for the Environment into negotiations over the city's budget and, by appearing to gain concessions, seemed to win the political battle. The rate-capped councils mounted a united campaign up to the deadline for making a rate when they capitulated. Normally, the Conservatives control the overwhelming majority of county councils. Their control was eroded by the rise of the SDP–Liberal Alliance: after the 1985 elections, 25 of the 46 English and Welsh county councils had no party in overall control. The new urban left flourished in metropolitan areas.[31] It was not content merely to oppose government policy. It also wanted to demonstrate that socialism could work and introduced local enterprise boards to counter unemployment, the effects of recession and regional decline.

The government conceded that there had been 'a worsening of the relationship between central government and even the moderate and responsible local authorities'.[32] Its response to the campaign waged against abolition by the GLC and the MCCs was less temperate. It appointed the Widdicombe Committee to inquire into the practices and procedures governing the conduct of local authority business. The inquiry was announced at the Conservative Party Conference and was widely seen as an attack on political advertising by Labour-controlled councils. The Committee recovered from this inauspicious start to produce an authoritative report documenting the politicisation of local government, the diversity of local politics and the *absence* of political abuses.[33] Confronted with evidence rather than rumour and cautious recommendations rather than retaliatory measures, the government deferred action pending a third term of office. Post-1986 local government affairs in general, not just local finance, were in limbo.

Differentiation

Local government's position as the pre-eminent governmental institution beyond Whitehall was challenged by the Conservative government which by-passed local authorities in favour of non-departmental public bodies. The MSC was preferred to local education authorities as the vehicle for improving vocational education in schools. In the inner cities the government preferred enterprise zones, free ports, urban development corporations and, the Financial Institutions Group to local authorities as the means of economic regeneration. The abolition of the GLC and the MCCs produced a whole crop of new agencies. The objectives of contracting-out include the increased involvement of the private sector in service provision (see below).

The government also sought to transform its relations with the range of public bodies beyond Whitehall. Several attempts were made to improve the efficiency of such bodies as the NHS through the introduction of contracting-out, performance indicators and general managers. Public corporations were privatised.[34]

If these changing relations between the government and quasi-governmental agencies are not documented here their importance should not be underestimated. Few policy areas are the domain of a single agency. Organisational interdependence is ubiquitous. Effective policy implementation requires inter-organisational co-operation. By proliferating agencies, by-passing local government and restructuring its relationship with non-departmental public bodies, the government fostered obstacles to co-operation and increased policy slippage. The range of agencies involved in the delivery of services increased substantially. The warrior style of the Prime Minister and the predeliction for commands over consultation were linked to structural differentiation which dissipated authority between agencies.

It would be foolhardy to deny that the thrust of the legislation between 1983 and 1987 was centralising but, equally, the capacity of the centre to realise its objectives should not be overestimated. Conservative policies contained the seeds of their own ineffectiveness. The system was complex, ambiguous, unstable and confused. Moreover, after retaliating for the failures of the first Parliament, the government lost its sense of direction. Policy towards local government lay in limbo. Local authorities were battered, bowed but not yet broken. The 'revolution' was around the corner of the next election.

FROM 1987 TO THE 1990s: REVOLUTION

The government and especially Mrs Thatcher displayed an almost morbid fascination with the low politics of local government finance. Few premiers have so willingly and so frequently become embroiled in local issues. Most have seen such interventions as high risk with a low rate of political return. After two Parliaments Mrs Thatcher's willingness to intervene was undiminished. If anything, the legislative programme became broader in scope. The narrow fixation on local expenditure gave way to a set of broader themes designed to restructure local government. As before, I focus on the distinctive themes of the government's programme: namely, accountability, competition, consumerism, and managerialism. There is one important difference from earlier sections. The effects of this legislation are only beginning to emerge. Inevitably, therefore, I cannot describe the actual effects of government policy and I must speculate on the likely outcome.

Accountability

'Cuts' in local expenditure are no longer the dominant theme. Accountability is the order of the day. To quote the Green Paper, the poll tax aims
'to make local authorities more accountable to their electors' by ensuring
'that the local electors know what the costs of their local services are, so
that armed with this knowledge they can influence the spending decisions
of their council through the ballot box'.[35] The Local Government Finance Act 1988 abolishes domestic rates and replaces them with a flat-
rate charge paid by all adults. The non-domestic or business rate is
replaced by the uniform business rate set by the centre. The grant system
has been (ostensibly) simplified and renamed the Revenue Support
Grant. In theory, this grant system will be more stable than its predecessors
with the amount of grant fixed in advance and not changed during the
year. The Act also introduces a range of minor changes: for example,
local authorities must appoint a professional accountant as chief financial
officer and (s)he must report instances of financial misconduct to the
council and the auditor.

The search for greater accountability has not been limited to local
government finance. The Education Reform Act 1988 gives parents more
control over schools. Governors are given responsibility for school
budgets and the appointment and dismissal of staff. Financial responsibility in the management of schools is delegated from the local education
authority (LEA) to the governors. If they wish, parents can run their
school and opt-out from LEA control (see below). The Local Government
and Housing Act 1989 prevents councils subsidising council house rents.
This move to 'affordable rents', like the poll tax, reinforces the link
between receiving and paying for a service.

The immediate consequences of the poll tax have been there for all to
see: demonstrations, backbench disquiet, poor government performance
in the opinion polls and (with rare exceptions) defeat in local elections.
The unpopularity of the tax is obvious. The extent of the government's
problems is less widely appreciated.

First, the full impact of the new system has not yet been felt, because
it is being phased in. The effects of the poll tax are ameliorated by a set
of transitional arrangements, or safety nets, which have served, for
example, to reduce bills in London. The uniform business rate, also
known as the national non-domestic rate, was based on a rating revalua-
tion which led to substantial increases in several areas of the country.
However, the government placed a ceiling in the total yield of the tax so

that it did not exceed the amount raised in 1989–90. The full impact of both changes will not be felt until 1994.

Secondly, the administrative effectiveness and costs of the new system remain to be seen. Each county or metropolitan district and London borough has to set up a community charge register. The tax will be paid by some 38 million individuals. The size of the registers and the total number of transactions is enormous, far greater than for the rates. Local authorities estimate that they will need an additional 17,000 staff to run the new system and that it will cost an additional £200 million per annum to administer. Enforcing registration and payment are a further cost. Houses do not pack a suitcase and move, people do. The problem of population mobility will probably be acute in the conurbations. Tony Travers has estimated that a 5 per cent failure to register/pay will add £13.15 per person to poll tax bills.[36]

Thirdly, the government is pursuing conflicting objectives. Under the new system up to 75 per cent of the total income of local authorities is decided by the centre. Between 25 and 37 per cent of total local authority income will come from the poll tax. As a result, and in theory, the government is in a position to exercise considerable downward pressure on local expenditure. Just to make sure, local authorities with 'excessive' poll taxes will be capped. In theory, poll tax clarifies the link between services and paying for them, encouraging electors to remove profligate Labour councils from office. However, in case electors either fail to spot the link between services and poll tax bills or, in an aberrant moment, vote for high levels of expenditure, the paternalistic government will step in and remedy the oversight by setting the poll tax at the 'correct' level. Accountability is the objective of the poll tax, provided electors do not vote for increased expenditure.

Finally, the new system is not only transitional, it is also unstable. The government will continue to use it for political ends. The Association of County Councils (ACC) is the respectable voice of local government at the national level. When the government announced its views of the likely levels of poll tax the ACC pointed out that the government 'seriously underestimates the actual cost of maintaining local government services at their present level'.[37] The consequences of this under-estimate was to make poll tax bills seem excessive. The government scored a political own goal. With a general election looming, it will not make the same mistake again. Grant will be manipulated to minimise poll tax levels. The 'services-payment' link will be obscured and financial stability will remain a chimera.

Amidst this flurry of change and political furore, there remained the simple intractable fact that haunted Conservative pronouncements throughout the 1980s: local current expenditure continued to rise in real terms.

Competition

The government has always favoured contracting-out and an increased role for the private sector in the provision of public services: for example, Wandsworth is a London borough often lauded by Conservative ministers for its pioneering and extensive use of contracting-out. Between 1981–3, 138 councils actively considered contracting-out but only 11 major contracts were signed. Thereafter interest declined dramatically.[38] The government was determined to legislate but, as with so much else, legislation was delayed. The second wave of activity had to await the Local Government Act 1988 which requires competition for refuse collection, street cleaning, catering, the cleaning of buildings, grounds maintenance and vehicle maintenance.

What are the effects of contracting-out? Walsh concludes that: 'there are large savings to be made ... some of which will come from reducing pay and conditions, some from new methods of working and some from increasing the pace of work and reducing the total labour input'.[39] In sum, competition cuts costs. However, it does not necessarily increase the role of the private sector. Ascher shows that the majority of contracts in the NHS were awarded to in-house labour forces and Painter has identified an identical trend in the first round of competitive tendering in local government.[40]

Consumerism

Allied to the notions of accountability and competition is the conception of citizens as customers, not as clients. Customers not only pay for their services – the link to accountability – they are also demanding and if not satisfied can go elsewhere – the link to competition. Local authorities should be responsive and recognise that 'quality of service demands closeness to customers and citizens'.[41]

The government applauds such sentiments and several pieces of legislation enhance citizens' choice. The Housing Act 1980 gives tenants the right to buy their council house. The Housing Act 1988 extends tenants' choice, giving them the right to choose a landlord other than the local authority. The Griffiths Report on care in the community proposed that local authorities should manage 'packages of care' combining private-sector and voluntary-sector provision with the NHS and local government.[42] The Education Reform Act 1988 also enhances parental choice. LEAs can no longer limit admissions to particular schools. Parents can choose between LEA schools, City Technology Colleges (CTCs) and Grant Maintained Schools (GMSs). CTCs are new schools created in partnership with the private sector which have curricula emphasising science and technology. GMSs are schools which have opted out of LEA control in response to parental wishes and which are funded directly by the centre.

Consumer choice has had some marked successes such as the sale of council houses and the substantial growth in private sector provision, for example for the elderly. The latest packages do not seem to offer the same prospects. The CTCs have opened but private sector support has been conspicuously inadequate, necessitating a massive injection of government funds. Opting-out is still rare and tends to involve schools threatened with closure because of falling school rolls. To date, tenants have voted to remain with local authority landlords. The government's response to the Griffiths Report was long delayed, presumably because it was reluctant to concede that local authorities should play the key role. As additional responsibilities will increase local expenditure and, as a consequence, poll tax bills, further delays cannot be ruled out. However, consumerism has developed a head of steam of its own. Even if the government's specific proposals have limited impact, it is likely to become a feature of local authority management. For example, improved housing management is one way of persuading tenants to retain the local authority as landlord.

Managerialism

Managerialism is a persistent and consistent feature of Conservative policy to the public sector. It has affected all alike: NHS, civil service, local government.[43] Perhaps the major innovation during the life of the first Parliament was the creation of the Audit Commission for Local Authorities in England and Wales in 1982. Its advocacy of the '3Es' of economy, efficiency and effectiveness has been a feature of the local government landscape ever since.

The government revisited the subject of the conduct of local authority business in its response to the Widdicombe Report[44] and in the Local

Government and Housing Act 1989. In drafting the Act, the findings of the Widdicombe Report were ignored when they conflicted with the government's preconceptions. The recommendations of the report were adopted only when convenient. Two themes pervade the Act: curbing politicisation and safeguards against political misconduct. Thus, attendance allowance for councillors is restricted; twin-tracking – or the employment of a councillor in another local authority – is severely curtailed; the strict pro-rata representation of political parties on all council committees and sub-committees is prescribed; and co-opted members of council committees are not allowed to vote (except of course, magistrates and church representatives). To guard against misconduct, the Act adopts a divide and rule strategy, requiring that every council appoint an officer responsible for financial probity, an officer responsible for legal propriety and one responsible for management co-ordination. It is possible that 'loony left' councils will think again if so advised by these powerful officials, but it is a doubtful solution to a non-problem. In sum, the government has extolled the virtues of a business-like approach but it has only tinkered with the management of local government whilst curbing its politicisation. However tentative recent steps, the '3Es' remain a constant pressure on local authorities.

Differentiation

Strengthening the role of governors, tenants' choice, CTCs and opting-out are all examples of by-passing local government. Contracting-out could increase the role of the private sector. Care packages envisage a reduced role for local authorities as service providers and the involvement of a range of agencies, public and private. The Housing Act 1988 seeks to increase the size of the private rented sector, to enhance the role of Housing Associations in the provision of housing and management of council estates, and to create Housing Action Trusts to take over and improve dilapidated council estates and then sell them either to the occupants or another landlord. Allied to the fragmentation of the government of metropolitan areas the overall trend is clear: in place of the all-purpose local authority, the government is creating differentiated service-delivery systems. This fragmentation is a by-product of a range of policies and it is only partially a product of design and intent. The consequences have yet to emerge. It is a key element in the uncertain future of the 1990s.

ASSESSMENT, EXPLANATION AND THE FUTURE

Assessment

Hindsight is invaluable. It makes it possible to identify trends and patterns, to sit outside the hurly-burly of events. From the first Parliament it is clear that the government sought to control the expenditure of individual local authorities and that the several reprises of policy simply multiplied unintended consequences. Frustrated by such failures, the government retaliated, abolishing and capping 'overspenders' to discover that it still had not achieved its goal of cutting local expenditure. Instability, ambiguity and confusion, not 'cuts', were the products of its actions. The relationship between central and local government was a policy mess. No level of government could attain its objectives. A stand-off ensued in which the government rethought its strategy and returned with a 'revolutionary' programme of reform.

If the government has failed to achieve its major objectives, if the overall result is a policy mess, none the less the record is not one of unrelieved gloom. Elements of the government's several policies have been successful. For example, its ideological message about the virtues of consumer choice and of competition has had some impact. The government has also derived marked political benefits from policies such as the sale of council houses. The outcome of the 'revolutionary' programme is unclear. The record does not inspire confidence. The prognosis has to be cautious, however, reflecting not only the fact that the government has had some success but also its persistence.

The weaknesses and problems of individual policies have already been noted. It is also instructive to note the contradictions in the programme of policies. There are arguments to support the conclusion that the reforms will be centralising. Up to 75 per cent of local authority income is now centrally determined. Similarly there seems to be a centralising trend in particular policy areas: for example, the introduction of the national curriculum in education. But there is equally clear evidence of decentralisation. A prime objective of the poll tax is to make councils accountable to their local electorate. The introduction of local management schemes in education decentralises financial management to schools and their governors. The government has proliferated agencies and thereby increased its problems of co-ordination and control. It could be argued that the strategy is to erode the powers of local government by centralising some functions (for example, the national curriculum) and decentralising others to markets or citizens (such as school finances). But the evidence for this interpretation is also contradictory. For example, local authorities have been given increased responsibilities for both child care and community care. The reason for this catalogue of contradictions is as simple as it is important. I have tried to describe recent changes in a systematic way, but consistency is not a feature of the government's programme. I have imposed a set of *ex post facto* rationalisations on a disparate and at times contradictory set of policies. Severally and individually none of the Acts post-1987 follows a consistent or simple set of principles,[45] a point demonstrated by the catalogue of contradictions.

Explanation[46]

In order to understand the likely outcome of the local government reforms of the 1980s it is necessary to explore the interaction between national economic problems, party ideology, party politics, bureaucratic tradition and bureaucratic politics.

Interventions in IGR do not reflect the government's concern with the state of local government but with the perceived imperatives of national economic management. In the case of the Conservative government, concern with inflation, the public sector borrowing requirement and the level of public expenditure shaped policy on local government. Although the Labour Party may have had a similar definition of the economic problem between 1975–9, the Conservative Party's response to Britain's relative economic decline was distinctively shaped by ideology. The control of local expenditure may have been a long-standing concern of the Treasury, but the policies on privatisation and the poll tax and the scale of contracting-out are distinctively Conservative. They also reflect the thinking of the New Right and its various think-tanks. Economic problems provided the stimulus to intervene. Party ideology shaped the form and extent of that intervention. Political parties give expression to ideology and are a major source of policy initiation, a counterweight to the inertia of Whitehall and established interests. They are also the focal point of conflict. Conservative policies have politicised and polarised IGR. The Labour Party has a majority on a substantial and increasing proportion of local councils. Local government has been simultaneously an area in which the electoral fortunes of the Labour Party have been revived, the test bed for socialist policies and the main source of opposition to the government. Local government has been a pawn in this increasingly polarised national party political arena.

The Conservative Party may have initiated a range of policies but intent and result diverged markedly in the process of implementation.[47] The government either did not anticipate or ignored the constraints imposed by the dual polity and by policy networks. The dual polity exemplifies the non-executant tradition of administration and the political insulation of centre from locality. The government was determined to intervene and to control individual local authorities. It adopted a command or bureaucratic operating code. Either it failed to understand or it chose to ignore the simple fact that British government is differentiated and disaggregated: the unitary state is a multiform maze of interdependencies. As a result, it lacked the hands-on means to impose its policies: the organisational infrastructure of field agents to supervise implementation. It also politicised relationships with local government thereby eroding the latter's 'responsibility ethic' or predisposition to conform to government expenditure guidelines.[48] Failure was built into the original policy design.

To compound the problem, the professional-bureaucratic complexes at the heart of British government – the policy networks – were a brake on the government's ambitions. Policy-making in British government is dominated by function-specific networks comprising central departments, professions and other key interests. Outside interests are institutionalised in government, relationships are routinised, the policy agenda is stable and conservative with a small 'c', and policy change is incremental. These networks, especially the professions, were 'handbagged' by the Thatcher government. Unfortunately, their co-operation was integral to the effective implementation of policy. A pattern of authoritative announcement by the centre followed by policy slippage in implementation became all too common. The dynamic conservatism of the policy networks illustrates the recurrent tension in British government between authoritative decision-making and interdependence.

The history of local government is compounded of multiple contradictions – economic, political and organisational. Monocausal explanations are inadequate. Policy-making for local government has generated a policy mess because of the failure to appreciate that disaggregation, differentiation, interdependence and policy networks are central characteristics of the British polity. Given the record of the first two Parliaments, the contradictions in the government's post-1987 programme, and the range of constraints on central initiatives, what is the future for local government?

The Future

Four scenarios can be identified: centralisation, the contract authority, community government and differentiation.

The *centralisation* scenario has been widely rehearsed. In brief, the 'New Leviathan' has been born. The centre now controls a huge proportion of local income. It dictates what is taught in schools. It abolishes, sells or by-passes the local services it does not like. Local government will atrophy, becoming an administrative agent of the centre.

The *contract* authority is the ideal of the New Right.[49] Local authorities cease to provide services directly. They contract both with the centre and within the locality for their provision. The role of local government is to manage contracts and regulate contractors. Services are provided by whomsoever can provide the best service at least cost – be that central agency, private sector, NHS or voluntary organisation.

The *community government* scenario envisages a revival of the pre-eminence of local government as the institution of government beyond Whitehall.[50] It seeks to create a new partnership with citizens based on a strategic role for local government, responsiveness in service delivery and strengthened local accountability. It is government by the community in that it seeks to decentralise services and run them with and through a range of agencies. It is government for the community in that local government does not manage a series of separate services but identifies issues of concern to the whole community.

The *differentiation* scenario predicts an extension of institutional fragmentation, a pattern of decision-making best characterised as disjointed incrementalism, and sub-optimal policy outcomes.[51] It encompasses elements from all the previous scenarios but concludes that no one scenario will predominate. Service delivery systems become ever more complex with attendant loss in comprehensibility, effectiveness and accountability.

These scenarios have been briefly sketched and space precludes a detailed exposition. Hopefully, it is clear that the future of local government is not preordained. Above all, as I have consistently argued, the term 'centralisation' does not begin to capture trends in the 1980s. Centralisation increased at the same time as the government's capacity to deliver services declined. Centralisation coexisted with the fragmentation of policy-making between policy networks and the proliferation of agencies beyond Whitehall.

If it is to be created, the contract authority will require at least another Parliament for the Conservatives. Local authorities will manage packages of services delivered by a variety of agencies. Local services will not necessarily be delivered by local government. But the systems of service delivery will be mixed, not conforming to any one pattern, and local government will remain the fulcrum.

The combination of a Labour government and economic growth may foster community government. I am not optimistic. At best, the centre is 'schizophrenic'[52] about local government. At worst, the economic and political interests of the government of the day, Conservative or Labour, override any putative commitment to 'local government'; central altruism is rare. I incline to the differentiation scenario of an ever more fragmented, complex and unaccountable system. It describes the end-product of a decade of intervention whilst making no assumptions about either the consistency of purpose of governments or their altruism.

Whichever future awaits local government, the final, ironic word must lie with Michael Heseltine, the man who started the government on its tortuous journey to a policy mess, and who in November 1990 was returned to the Environment Department to sort it out:

I have yet to be persuaded that, in order to discipline a limited number of defaulters, the government is wise to undertake a frontal change in local government finance which will extend its consequences to every constituency in England and Wales, with incalculable but not unpredictable effects.[53]

Now he tells us!

NOTES

* I would like to thank Keith Alderman (University of York) and Gerry Stoker (University of Essex) for their constructive comments on an earlier draft of this chapter.
1. See J. Benyon, 'Ten Years of Thatcherism', *Social Studies Review*, 4 (5), 1989, p. 177, and J. Stewart and G. Stoker (eds), *The Future of Local Government* (London: Unwin-Hyman, 1989) p. 2.
2. See for example T. Burgess and T. Travers, *Ten Billion Pounds: Whitehall's Takeover of the Town Halls* (London: Grant McIntyre, 1980). Other later examples include G. Jones and J. Stewart, *The Case for Local Government* (London: George Allen & Unwin, 1983) and M. Goldsmith and K. Newton, 'Central–Local Government Relations: the Irresitible Rise of Centralised Power', *West European Politics*, 6, 1983, pp. 216–33. A complete listing would be as long as it would be tedious. Centralisation is a new conventional wisdom on local government.
3. Stewart and Stoker, pp. 1–2 and 4.

4.　This term was employed in R. A. W. Rhodes, 'Continuity and Change in British Central–Local Relations: the Conservative Threat, 1979–83', *British Journal of Political Science*, 14, 1984, pp. 261–83.

5.　In chronological order they are: P. Dunleavy and R. A. W. Rhodes, 'Beyond Whitehall', in H. Drucker *et al.* (eds), *Developments in British Politics* (London: Macmillan, 1983) pp. 106–33; Rhodes, 'Continuity and Change'; P. Dunleavy and R. A. W. Rhodes, 'Government Beyond Whitehall', in H. Drucker *et al.* (eds), *Developments in British Politics 2* (London: Macmillan, 1986) pp. 107–43, and *Developments in British Politics 2*, rev. edn, 1988, pp. 107–43; and R. A. W. Rhodes, *Beyond Westminster and Whitehall* (London: Unwin-Hyman, 1988).

6.　J. G. Bulpitt, *Territory and Power in the United Kingdom* (Manchester: Manchester University Press, 1983) p. 3.

7.　For a more thorough account of the postwar period, see R. A. W. Rhodes, ' "A Squalid and Politically Corrupt Process"?: Intergovernmental Relations in the Post-War Period', *Local Government Studies,* 11 (6), 1985, pp. 35–57; and Rhodes, *Beyond Westminster and Whitehall*, ch. 5.

8.　See for example Committee of Enquiry into Local Government Finance (the Layfield Committee), *Report*, Cmnd 6453 (London: HMSO, 1976).

9.　See R. A. W. Rhodes, *The National World of Local Government* (London: George Allen & Unwin, 1986) p. 149.

10.　The best survey of housing policy can be found in P. Malpass and A. Murie, *Housing Policy and Practice*, 3rd edn (London: Macmillan, 1990).

11.　Ibid., ch. 4.

12.　For a review of the key cases, see O. Lomas, 'Law', in S. Ranson, G. Jones and K. Walsh (eds), *Between Centre and Locality* (London: George Allen & Unwin, 1985) pp. 81–99.

13.　Jones and Stewart, *The Case for Local Government*, p. 37.

14.　E. M. Davies, J. G. Gibson, C. H. Game and J. D. Stewart, *Grant Characteristics and Central–Local Relations* (London: Social Science Research Council, 1983) p. 251.

15.　B. Hardy, G. Wistow and R. A. W. Rhodes, 'Policy Networks and the Implementation of Community Care Policy for People with Mental Handicaps', *Journal of Social Policy*, 19, 1990, pp. 141–68.

16.　See N. Flynn, S. Leach and C. Vielba, *Abolition or Reform? The GLC and the Metropolitan County Councils* (London: George Allen & Unwin, 1985), pp. 8–11; and A. Forrester, S. Lansley and R. Pauley, *Beyond our Ken: A Guide to the Battle for London* (London: Fourth Estate, 1985) ch. 4.

17.　*Streamlining the Cities*, Cmnd 9063 (London: HMSO, 1983) p. 5.

18.　S. James, 'The New Pattern of London Government', *Public Administration*, 68, 1990, pp. 493–4.

19.　B. O'Leary, 'Why Was the GLC Abolished?', *International Journal of Urban and Regional Research*, 11 (2), 1987, pp. 193–217.

20.　M. Hebbert and T. Travers (eds), *The London Government Handbook* (London: Cassell, 1988) pp. 196–7.

21.　W. A. Robson, *The Government and Misgovernment of London*, 2nd edn (London: George Allen & Unwin, 1948) p. 172.

22.　These several criticisms are paraphrased from Hebbert and Travers, *The London Government Handbook*, pp. 188–91; and C. Game and S. Leach, 'The Abolition of Metropolitan Governments', mimeo (Birmingham: INLOGOV, 1989).

23.　C. Skelcher and S. Leach, 'Resource Choice and the Abolition Process', *Local Government Studies*, 16 (3), 1990, p. 41.

24.　Hebbert and Travers, *The London Government Handbook*, p. 187.

25.　*Paying for Local Government*, Cmnd 9714 (London: HMSO, 1986).

26. P. Jenkins, *Mrs Thatcher's Revolution* (London: Pan Books, 1989) p. 280.
27. H. Young, *One of Us* (London: Macmillan, 1989) p. 521.
28. A. Wildavsky, *Budgeting* (Boston, Mass.: Little, Brown, 1975) pp. 144–5.
29. Space precludes an account of IGR in the constituent nations of the UK but see Rhodes, *Beyond Westminster and Whitehall*; A. Midwinter, *The Politics of Local Spending* (Edinburgh: Mainstream Publishing, 1984); and M. Goldsmith, 'Managing the Periphery in a Period of Fixed Stress', in M. Goldsmith (ed.), *New Research in Central–Local Relations* (Aldershot: Gower, 1986) pp. 152–72.
30. Audit Commission for Local Authorities in England and Wales, *The Impact on Local Authorities' Economy, Efficiency and Effectiveness of the Block Grant Distribution System* (London: HMSO, 1984); and Committee of Public Accounts, Seventh Report: *Operation of the Rate Support Grant System*, Session 1985–86, HC 47 (London: HMSO, 1985).
31. See J. Gyford, *The Politics of Local Socialism* (London: George Allen & Unwin, 1985); and M. Boddy and C. Fudge (eds), *Local Socialism?* (London: Macmillan, 1984).
32. *Paying for Local Government*, Cmnd 9714, p. 5.
33. Committee of Inquiry into the Conduct of Local Government (the Widdicombe Committee), *Report*, Cmnd 9797 (London: HMSO, 1986).
34. For a brief survey see Rhodes, *Beyond Westminster and Whitehall*, pp. 120–31. For more detail see R. Klein, *The Politics of the NHS*, 2nd edn (London: Longman, 1989); and R. Frazer (ed.), *Privatization: The UK Experience and International Trends* (London: Longman, 1988).
35. *Paying for Local Government*, Cmnd 9714, pp. 9 and vii.
36. T. Travers, 'Community Charge and Other Financial Changes', in Stewart and Stoker (eds), *The Future of Local Government*, p. 24.
37. Association of County Councils, 'Community Charge Statement', *Gazette*, 82 (11), 1990, p. 285.
38. K. Ascher, *The Politics of Privatization: Contracting Out Public Services* (London: Macmillan, 1987) pp. 222–3.
39. K. Walsh, 'Competition and Service in Local Government', in Stewart and Stoker (eds), *The Future of Local Government*, p. 44.
40. See Ascher, *The Politics of Privatization*, pp. 187 and 298; and J. Painter, *The Future of the Public Sector: Seconds Out, Round Two* (Milton Keynes: The Open University, mimeo, March 1989) p. 13.
41. Local Government Training Board, *Getting Closer to the Public* (Luton: LGTB, 1987) pp. 4–5. See also J. Stewart, *Understanding the Management of Local Government* (London: Longman, 1988) chs 5–7.
42. Sir R. Griffith, *Community Care: An Agenda for Action* (London: HMSO, 1988).
43. See for example L. Metcalfe and S. Richards, *Improving Public Management*, 2nd edn (London: Sage, 1990).
44. *The Conduct of Local Authority Business: The Government Response to the Report of the Widdicombe Committee of Inquiry*, Cmnd 433 (London: HMSO, 1988).
45. On this point see also Stewart and Stoker, *The Future of Local Government*, p. 2; and H. Glennerster, A. Power and T. Travers, 'A New Era for Social Policy: a New Enlightenment or a New Leviathan?', The Welfare State Programme: Suntory-Toyota International Centre for Economics and Related Disciplines, Discussion Paper WSP/39 (London: London School of Economics, 1989) p. 48.
46. The analysis is an abbreviated version of Rhodes, *Beyond Westminster and Whitehall*, pp. 48–9 and 371–87.
47. A. Wildavsky, *The Art and Craft of Policy Analysis* (London: Macmillan, 1980) p. 16, describes policies as hypotheses. Conservative policy could have failed, therefore, because its hypotheses were incorrect. Enoch Powell has commented:

'By all means limit Exchequer grants and Government loans: but every monetarist knows that the rates cannot cause inflation and councils cannot print money. So why set every elected council by the ears from one end of Britain to the other?' (Cited in Jones and Stewart, *The Case for Local Government*, p. 61.) In other words, monetarist policy does *not* require control of current expenditure, only capital expenditure! However, any detailed discussion of the theory underlying government policies would have to include, although it would not be limited to, an appraisal of New Right theory. Such a review would take this chapter too far afield.

48. G. Bramley and M. Stewart, 'Implementing Public Expenditure Cuts', in S. Barrett and C. Fudge (eds), *Policy and Action* (London: Methuen, 1981) p. 60.

49. N. Ridley, *The Local Right: Enabling Not Providing* (London: Centre for Policy Studies, 1988) .

50. J. Stewart and G. Stoker, *From Local Administration to Community Government*, Fabian Research Series 351 (London: Fabian Society, 1988).

51. Rhodes, *Beyond Westminster and Whitehall*, pp. 406–13.

52. M. Kogan, *The Politics of Education* (Harmondsworth: Penguin, 1971) p. 171.

53. M. Heseltine, *Where There's A Will* (London: Hutchinson, 1987) p. 304.

6. The Community and Britain: The Changing Relationship between London and Brussels

Lord Clinton-Davis

It was Philip Larkin, no stranger to Hull University, who said, 'As for Hull, I like it because it's so far away from everywhere else. On the way to nowhere, as somebody put it.' He also said, 'I wouldn't mind seeing China if I could come back the same day. I hate being abroad. Generally speaking, the further one gets from home, the greater the misery.' I cannot help thinking that those words mirror to a large extent the feelings that Mrs Thatcher has about the European Community.

In addressing the topic of the changing relationship between Britain and the European Community I thought that I would approach it – I hope not too presumptuously – rather as did Gaugin in his famous painting: 'Where did we come from? Where are we? Where are we going?'. So I propose to start by recounting a little of the history of Britain and its relations with the rest of Europe since the end of the Second World War; then examine the reasons why we are starting to see a change in some of our attitudes towards Europe; and finally – to do that which is most dangerous – to look ahead towards and beyond the magical date of 1992 and to see what more we can do to try to influence events.

ORIGINS OF EUROPEAN UNION

Any examination of the relationship between Britain and the rest of Europe – and in making that distinction I must suggest that this country has still not accommodated itself to being a fully engaged member of the European Community (EC) – must take us back to the postwar scene and the situation in which Britain found herself in 1945.

Vast areas of Europe, including the British Isles, had suffered destruction or damage and only the neutral states of Sweden and Switzerland remained untouched. Particularly affected were Europe's communications networks – roads, railways, bridges, marshalling yards, sea ports – and everywhere factories had been severely damaged, reducing output to one-third of what it had been in 1938. In France almost a fifth of its houses and two-thirds of its railway stock had been destroyed. In Germany, two-fifths of the buildings in the 50 largest cities had been destroyed, with Frankfurt, Düsseldorf and Berlin regarded as virtually uninhabitable. Elsewhere, from Denmark and Norway in the north to Italy and Greece in the south, countries had been occupied or overtaken by the Allied advances and a trail of destruction left in their wake. Nearly one-third of Italy's national assets were destroyed, Norway's merchant fleet was in ruins and Denmark virtually bankrupt as a nation.

Added to the material cost and, of course, infinitely more important, was the destruction of human life on an unprecedented scale: six million Jews slaughtered in the Nazi concentration camps as part of their evil design to eliminate the entire Jewish population of Europe; two million French transported to Germany; four million German soldiers killed or reported missing; countless civilians killed or injured. Many citizens of those countries that had been occupied, in spite of the efforts of the resistance movements, were broken both financially and in spirit, and yet had to face the superhuman task of postwar reconstruction. On an international scale foreign trade was virtually at a standstill, sources of invisible earnings had vanished, and although America was in a position to supply Europe with all of its needs, there was neither the cash nor credit available to make this possible.

It was against this background that some of the earliest thinking about the future shape of Europe had already taken place. It must be emphasised that at the end of the war Britain remained one of the great powers. Although Britain was a small island, our spheres of influence included relationships with the old Empire (later to become the Commonwealth), with the United States and with the rest of Europe. And we had, of course, played a significant part in the destruction of Nazism; albeit at enormous cost.

The horror of what nation states were capable of doing to each other, during the course of two world wars in the space of just 20 years, had a profound influence on the postwar thinking of politicians and statesmen. Indeed, many of the origins of the movement of postwar European unification can be traced to the underground resistance movements and governments in exile, several of whom had their organisations based in London – among them, of course, France's General de Gaulle.

PLANS FOR EUROPEAN RECOVERY

It was an American impetus that helped give shape to the first practical attempt at setting up a supranational European organisation for the purposes of co-ordinating the European recovery programme. Before 1947, when American Secretary of State George Marshall put forward details of the plan that was to bear his name, a number of national planning organisations had been set up – in France, Belgium, Italy and other countries which were already benefiting from various forms of aid, first under the Roosevelt lease-lend programme and later through the newly-established United Nations Relief and Recovery Agency. Following a conference at Bretton Woods in 1944 an International Bank for Reconstruction and Development was set up, with further assistance from the International Monetary Fund (IMF), with a view to helping European countries devastated by war back on to the path of recovery. It should be recalled that such aid, and indeed the Marshall Plan, was offered to all countries of both East and West Europe, but eventually was declined by the former who gradually retreated behind the Iron Curtain that was to remain a symbol of East-West Cold War relations for several decades to come.[1]

It was American assistance on a co-ordinated approach to West European recovery that led to the creation of the Organisation for European Economic Recovery to administer the Marshall Plan, under which a further $23 billion of American aid was pumped into Europe between 1947 and 1952, by which time the economies of Western Europe were well on their way towards full economic health.

The importance of the OEEC lies in its role in convincing European politicians of the need for mutual economic co-operation. Although originally set up to fulfil a specific need, after its twelve-year life OEEC was transformed in 1960 into the OECD (Organisation for Economic Co-operation and Development), and the United States and Canada became full members. With the entry of Japan in 1964 its purely European role was diluted, paving the way for the establishment of new European institutions.

TOWARDS INTEGRATION

The question was then asked, what sort of Europe do we want? There was of course the example of America, which led politicians such as Winston Churchill to talk about a 'United States of Europe' – with an elected Parliament, a European Court and a joint European army – while France's Jean Monnet was already proclaiming that Europe 'must federate or perish'. It is not surprising that, in this heady atmosphere and spurred on by the need to give practical effect to the imaginative Marshall Plan in the rehabilitation and reorganisation of Europe, a number of new European groupings emerged during the immediate postwar decade.

The Churchill-inspired broad European movement met in conference at The Hague and this led to the foundation of the Council of Europe – still Western Europe's largest international forum. Britain's support for the Council of Europe was not matched, however, by any marked enthusiasm for close co-operation. Europe had of necessity been brought closer together, at the instigation of the United States, for the purposes of administering the Marshall Plan. The Americans insisted that this should be on a European-wide and not a national basis and the OEEC was accordingly set up. But when a group of forward-thinking European statesmen – including Jean Monnet, director of the French plan, and his Foreign Minister Robert Schumann – put forward a plan for integrating Europe's coal and steel production, Britain's premier, Clement Attlee, was unenthusiastic. He and his newly elected Labour government were preoccupied with other vitally important issues: reconstructing Britain's own war-torn economy; the absorption of millions of servicemen and women into its peace-time economy, while avoiding the demoralising mass unemployment which followed the ending of the First World War; and in the establishment of Britain's welfare state. Attlee also pleaded this country's so-called special relationship with the United States and its commitments to the Commonwealth. And there was concern too about handing over control of the newly established nationalised industries to a supranational body. It would be misleading, however, to depict the Labour government as being indifferent to the plight of Europe. Foreign Secretary Ernest Bevin played a massive role in the renewal of German industry and the German trade union movement. He, indeed, was one of the authors of worker consultation and participation which has played so vital a role over the years in producing the so-called German economic miracle.

With the benefit of hindsight, it can certainly be argued now that most British politicians, in believing that Britain could 'go it alone', were living in a dream world, suffering perhaps – as Adlai Stevenson said of Dwight D. Eisenhower – 'from delusions of adequacy'. For there were clear signs already that Britain's role as a superpower could not match the strength of the United States and the USSR. Britain was also declining as a trading nation, its share of world trade dropping from 25 per cent before the war to 2 per cent in its aftermath. The country's severe difficulties were compounded by unrealistic commitments to the navy, the army of the Rhine and nuclear defence – involving expenditure of up to 8 per cent of its Gross Domestic Product against 2 per cent by Germany. All of this at a time when Germany's output was twice and France's one-and-a-half times that of Britain's. Already there were distinct signs that Britain was being left behind in Europe.

THE ECSC AND EURATOM

The Monnet Plan for the European Coal and Steel Community was warmly welcomed by Konrad Adenauer of West Germany, Alcide de Gasperi of Italy and Paul Henri Spaak of Belgium. These European statesmen realised only too well that two world wars had largely been fought over coal and steel, but Britain steadfastly refused to sign the Treaty of Paris in 1951, stating (and how often we would hear this phrase again) that Britain would consider joining 'when the time was right'!

The interesting thing about the ECSC is that for the first time in European history the concept of a High Authority was accepted. This was a supranational body, composed of international civil servants and backed by a European Court of Justice, which would oversee compliance with the provisions of the Treaty of Paris and which could take decisions that would affect all the member states, companies and individuals. There was even a common assembly to act as a check on the bureaucracy. Already institutions were being put in place that were later to become the European Commission and the European Parliament. No wonder so many in Britain were horrified that we too might be enmeshed in this emergence of a new European sovereignty and preferred to bask in the misleading evocations of a past grandeur.

In the field of European defence, although Britain had been a founder member of NATO in 1949 she was concerned about the concept of a combined European army and the permanent institutions needed to control it. But while France went to war in Indo-China and the United States in Korea, Germany was left largely uncommitted, except for the fact that it was promptly admitted to NATO, while at enormous cost to itself Britain agreed to station troops in Germany for a period of 50 years.

Meanwhile European politicians were looking at the future of nuclear power, and again invited Britain to join a proposed European body: Euratom. Once again Britain, fearful about sharing its atomic secrets with our European neighbours, declined the invitation. Nevertheless, the other six went ahead and, of course, the culmination of their deliberations was the signing in 1957 of the Treaty of Rome setting up the European Communities, incorporating the original ECSC, Euratom and a new Economic Community. The founder members were West Germany, France, Italy, Belgium, Holland and Luxembourg (the last three having come together in Europe's first customs union, Benelux, as early as 1948). Britain, however, stayed outside.

EFTA AND THE OUTER SEVEN

Within a few years Britain was to suffer the shockwaves of its East of Suez policies, the splitting of India and Pakistan and decolonisation elsewhere. Historians will recall Macmillan's famous 'winds of change' speech in South Africa which so aptly summarised the mood at the time. Looking towards Europe, however, Britain soon found that, helped by new institutions such as the European Investment Bank, the European Structural Funds and the Common Agricultural Policy (all set up in 1958), the six founder members of the European Community were starting to overtake Britain economically. Instead of reassessing its attitude towards the nascent European Communities, Britain further underlined its scepticism and distrust by being the prime mover in establishing a rival organisation – EFTA (the European Free Trade Area) – bringing together the outer seven comprising Sweden, Norway, Denmark, Switzerland, Austria, Portugal and Britain, in what many Europeans and, indeed, Americans saw as an attempt to undermine the emerging European Community.

BRITISH APPLICATIONS TO THE EEC

By the 1960s, however, Britain's options were already starting to diminish. South Africa withdrew from the Commonwealth, India and

Pakistan were at loggerheads, and accordingly British trade and investment started to turn towards Europe. By 1961 our first application to join the Community was submitted, necessitated, according to Harold Macmillan, 'by the need to preserve the power and strength of Britain in the world'. Edward Heath was our chief negotiator.

For its part, the EEC had already achieved many of its goals, including proposals for the establishment of a full customs union, and was looking favourably at the potential for enlargement. While there was slower progress in the area of political union, it was clear to Macmillan and Britain that the Community was rapidly emerging as a viable economic unity and Britain's position in the world would be greatly strengthened by being part of it rather than remaining outside. There was support for the British approach by some of the smaller Community states who saw in Britain a counterweight to the strengths of France and Germany. The climate overall appeared favourable.

But, as we all know, Britain's application was eventually rejected, vetoed in effect by France's President de Gaulle who remained convinced that Britain could not genuinely become a loyal member of the EC while retaining its economic and spiritual ties with the Commonwealth, the United States and EFTA. Britain's membership, de Gaulle argued, would lead to dilution of the Community or dominance by the United States or both.

By 1965 we had had a Unilateral Declaration of Independence by Rhodesia and the new Wilson government pragmatically submitted a further European application, modifying radically many of Britain's demands. De Gaulle, however, remained unconvinced and the application lapsed. Britain had to wait until the resignation of de Gaulle in 1969 and the Conservative election victory in 1970 before a third and this time even more watered-down application could be made. By the time Britain joined the Community in 1973, along with Ireland and Denmark, Europe was in the grip of the first oil crisis, Britain's economy was in serious trouble and there was widespread industrial unrest in the UK, culminating in the miners' strike of 1974 and the return of a minority Labour government.

DAWN OF FALSE HOPES

Britain's application in 1970 was very different from the invitations that had been extended to join the original six 20 years earlier. In the intervening decades Europe had forged ahead economically while Britain's economy had declined, together with any pretensions of being a front-ranking world power. Accordingly, our entry in 1973 was seen by many – not least by the then Conservative government – as a cure-all for Britain's many ills. Expectations were awakened that realistically could not be fulfilled. How much more prudent they would have been at least to recall the wise advice of Alexander Pope in a letter to John Gay: 'Blessed is he who expects nothing, for he shall never be disappointed.' It is not surprising that disillusionment eventually followed, compounded by the fact that the electorate had been denied any opportunity to cast its vote on the issue of membership, a constitutional issue of almost unprecedented magnitude.

It is here – in Britain's late arrival and the eventual referendum of 1975 which resulted in a two-to-one majority in favour of staying inside the Community – that we can trace the origins of Britain's ambivalence towards Europe which is still apparent today. By the mid-1970s we were a *de facto* but reluctant member of the club. In no way, however, did that deter us from trying to change the rules. In 1978, when the European Monetary System was proposed, Britain again only half-joined – staying outside the Exchange Rate Mechanism (ERM) – and arguing that it reduced our ability to devalue and could lead to unemployment.

But it was after Mrs Thatcher's election in 1979 that British nationalism let rip. The Prime Minister, laudably in many ways, was to go on and on 'demanding our money back' in the form of a £1 billion cut in Britain's contribution. The trouble was that she wanted to discuss scarcely anything else and her encounters with her European colleagues at successive summits were marked by her with all the gentility and diplomacy of a Mike Gatting at bay in South Africa.

It is true that a compromise, by no means the one demanded by Britain, was reached at Fontainbleu in 1984. Regrettably, however, the posturing, which did little for Anglo-European relations, did not stop there. For by 1985, hardly had the ink dried on Lord Cockfield's White Paper[2] on the Internal Market and Britain signed the Single European Act in 1986, than shrill cries were heard not simply from Britain's traditional anti-Common Marketeers but from the government itself, that the Single European Act – which Mrs Thatcher had only just signed – would transform the Common Market into a European Union, a super-state in which national sovereignty would be ceded to a centralised, semi-Marxist bureaucracy based in Brussels. These sentiments were mirrored in the now famous Thatcher speech in Bruges in 1988 and her nightmare of an 'Identikit Europe'.

BRITAIN OUT OF STEP

I have dwelt at some length on the events surrounding the foundation of the European Community since I think it is important to emphasise the background to the thinking of our European partners. Even the much maligned Common Agricultural Policy and its well-documented surpluses can be traced to genuine basic concerns about going hungry after the devastation of two world wars. It is this way of looking at Europe that needs to be understood when we come to examine the implications of the Single European Act, with its emphasis on mutual co-operation, a Social Charter and greater political union. It is in rejecting these wider implications of this philosophical approach to Europe and concentrating only on selected elements of the deregulated internal market that the present British government finds itself so often out of step with our Community partners.

For it is the political conflict over Europe and its future that has increasingly dominated the thinking of British governments, in particular with regard to monetary union and the wider social dimension. This has to be set against the practical experience of Community membership under the Wilson, Callaghan and Thatcher administrations, when for different reasons both industrialists and trade unionists have found themselves drawn increasingly into involvement in the European institutions. It is this experience, coupled with a transformation of the attitudes of the Left, that have brought about the significant changes in British attitudes to Europe and set them apart in many instances from official government attitudes.

The other catalyst for change has been the impact of the Single European Act, but here again we find the circumscribed attitude of the government, which sees Britain's contribution to the Common Market almost exclusively as opening up an area of unrestrained competition by the end of 1992 while it rejects the wider implications of the concept of a new, cohesive Europe, based on maximising the politics of consensus which has been developed by the Commission and the European Parliament. The approach of the government is based on a distortion or a fundamental misunderstanding of both the letter and intent of the Act to which Prime Minister Thatcher subscribed her name on behalf of the UK.

THE SINGLE EUROPEAN ACT

I am not suggesting that the Single European Act, and with it the new climate that will prevail after 1992, are not firmly founded upon economic necessity – a reaction to concerns about the technical and trading superiorities of America and the Far East. But there is a need to resolve and not to exacerbate conflict between the desire for liberalisation and the requirement to establish acceptable ground rules covering the environment, social policy, co-operative research and development, regional assistance, transport, harmonisation of technical standards, mutual recognition of national qualifications, and fiscal and monetary harmonisation. Unfortunately for those wanting to pick and choose only those bits of the Single European Act that suit their own narrow free-market aspirations there is no such luxury as a Europe *à la carte*.

As a study of the text of the Single European Act quickly reveals, this product of hard and complex negotiation is much more than a framework for implementing the so-called 1992 Programme. It is the design for the construction of a true Community, a Community combining to deal with problems which may not directly affect us in individual countries; using national resources to achieve rewards that will be internationally shared; taking decisions in the common good, when the benefits may accrue in another generation, in another century, in another place. The SEA is not, and never was intended to facilitate, the creation of just a common market.

Witness Title I of the Act which begins by recording the solemn declaration made in Stuttgart in June 1983 to transform relations as a whole among the member states into a European Union. It clearly expresses the parties' intention to implement European Union first on the basis of the Communities and secondly of European co-operation in the sphere of foreign policy. It further records that the parties are determined to ensure the smoother functioning of the Community institutions and to achieve the progressive realisation of Economic and Monetary Union, having regard in particular to the European Council's resolution on the introduction of the European Monetary System. In Title II we find details of the 'New Co-operation Procedure' to be applied to certain measures adopted under the Treaty; for the use of qualified majority voting (instead of unanimous agreement) on a variety of measures; for the progressive realisation of a single market by the end of 1992; and for European co-operation on monetary policy, social policy, economic and social cohesion, research and technological development, and on the preservation of the environment.

That, then, is the reality of the Single European Act – even if the details of the text come as a surprise to some commentators, perhaps even to one or two signatories! But even the most radical assessment of the Act must confirm that it sets out a framework for the more effective achievement of goals set by the founding fathers of the Community over 30 years ago and enshrined in the original Treaty of Rome. By signing the Single European Act the member states have finally ensured the effective establishment of the single market by means of legislative acts adopted on the basis of majority voting and establishing a sounder legal basis for European political co-operation at the same time as broadening the whole question of European defence.

It is in the light of the text of the Single European Act that we should study extensions of Commission thinking contained in documents such as the Delors Report on Economic and Monetary Union or the text of the Draft Social Charter, the latter derided by Mrs Thatcher as 'inspired by the values of Marxism and the class struggle'. The issues of monetary union and the European social dimension have increasingly emerged on the British political scene. In the case of the former, Prime Minister Thatcher appeared to be out of step with the CBI, the TUC, the Bank of England and her former Chancellor – to say nothing of most of her Cabinet minions; while the prospect of a fairer and more compassionate society with a more consensual approach to the making of decisions which affect our everyday lives finally persuaded trade unionists to embrace Frère Jacques Delors and his vision of a Peoples' Europe and of a Social Charter. It is pathetic to describe all this, as Mrs Thatcher did very frequently, as 'Socialism by the back door'.

Coming down to more practical levels, we in Britain are at last becoming more aware of Europe. Within industry and the trade unions there is a growing realisation that there are opportunities for Britain as a fully committed member of the Community. While some business people may be more concerned about the consequences than capable of grasping the opportunities offered by the single market, none of us can be unaware that our competitors from across the Channel are already active in Britain, even to the extent of successfully bidding for and winning public contracts for services such as street cleaning and school meals provision.

Coupled with a realisation of the business opportunities in a market of 329 million consumers there must be a transformation in Britain's attitude to the broader issues of the environment, pollution, nuclear safety, transport infrastructure, education, the role of women, working hours, wages and many other areas where the millions of Britons who travel abroad on holiday or business cannot fail to realise how far we lag behind many of our continental neighbours and that many of these are truly international issues and cannot be treated in isolation.

THE FUTURE – REALITY, IDEALISM AND SOME DIFFICULT QUESTIONS

Coming to the future, what is likely to happen to Britain's relationship with the EC in the next decade? No one, especially after the events of 1989–90, can safely forecast anything. But I do think that the way we respond to certain fundamental challenges will help us to shape that relationship.

First, there is the critical need, given added emphasis by the struggles of the people of Eastern Europe, to practise political pluralism, to remedy what has become known as 'the democratic deficit' in the functioning of the major Community institutions. To start with there is the Council of Ministers. Their affairs are conducted totally in secret, except for the record of the conclusions reached, thereby debarring Community citizens, even parliamentarians, from knowing anything about the debates that have gone on behind closed doors, debates that can vitally affect the future of millions of us. That, and sweeping aside so much of the secrecy which stifles freedom in our industrial, environmental and political policies, is vital if we are to become truly participative democracies.

Secondly, the EC, like any legal entity, can only function if there is respect for the rule of law – by complying with Community Regulations and Directives and judgements of the European Court of Justice. In the field of the environment alone, the European Commission has been obliged to initiate proceedings against member states in more than 400 cases. When the law-makers themselves treat the law with such contempt that is the worst possible abuse of democracy.

Thirdly, there is the need to strengthen and improve other major Community institutions, particularly the Commission and the Parliament. For Europe to function more effectively, its executive arm – *the Commission* – must be able to exercise its powers, particularly in situations demanding urgent action – such as the aftermath of Chernobyl or the rapidly changing scene in Eastern Europe – far more rapidly, comprehensively and effectively. Yet at present some member states (and notably Britain) are fearful of extending this competence and equally fearful of extending the capacity of the Parliament (as the only elected body in the constellation of European institutions) to hold the Commission more accountable.

Hence the refusal by the member states to face up to the fact that some parts of the Commission are clearly overworked and understaffed – the organisation numbers just 12,000, about a fifth being involved in translation: fewer probably than the local authority employs in Hull and less than Britain's 17,000-strong Department of Transport.

As to the Commissioners themselves, there must be a strong case for investing the President with the powers to allocate portfolios to the 17 individual Commissioners and to move them from one portfolio to another, again subject always to some accountability to the European Parliament. At present the College of 17 Commissioners has to be unanimous about the selection of responsibilities and, once in a position, there the Commissioner stays for the entirety of the four-year mandate.

It was Walter Hallstein, the Commission's first President, who envisaged the Commission as 'the guardian of the Treaties, the motor of the European Community, and the honest broker between member states'. The Commission declined from the mid-1960s when legal powers were usurped by the Council of Ministers and a succession of economic crises fostered more nationalistic attitudes among member states. Correspondingly the Commission tended to become more bureaucratic and the European ideal somewhat tarnished. As the Community grew in size there were fewer opportunities for finding consensus, the common ground of European politics.

Under the imaginative leadership of Jacques Delors there can be no doubt that the Commission has been rediscovering its role, but the changes I have suggested seem to be critical to reinforce its ability to deal with the vastly more complex problems that confront us today.

Fourthly, the new Co-operation Procedures outlined in the Single European Act have clearly enhanced the role and status of the *European Parliament*. It should have extended and real powers, *inter alia*: (a) to initiate legislation; (b) to be involved in the proceedings of the Council of Ministers – and I do not mean just a formal presence. It would certainly help too if the Parliament and its offices could be sited permanently in Brussels rather than in two, sometimes even three, locations.

There is much room for improvement too in the relationship between MEPs and MPs. At present MEPs are denied any special privileges of access to the House of Commons and its facilities, such as the research services. Indeed, it would be no exaggeration to say that they are regarded rather as pariahs. Contrast this with the situation in the Federal Republic where MEPs serve as non-voting members of parliamentary committees, providing an expertise on EC affairs which is usually not available to anything like the same degree elsewhere in the domestic Parliament. A similar cross-fertilisation of ideas and experience could only be of benefit to our own Parliament and its greater appreciation of EC policies.

Members of the UK Parliament, for their part, complain of the lack of early information coming from Brussels. Although both Houses have their committees to scrutinise European legislation, their approach is highly selective and many backbenchers find that European laws, albeit enacted by ministers from the member states in the Council of Ministers, have become a reality almost before they realise it.

Perhaps most important of all, the case for proportional representation in Euro-elections is, I think, overwhelming. It is practised in 11 of the 12 member states and even in part of the UK – Northern Ireland. The defence of the first-past-the-post system is scarcely sustained in this instance by praying-in-aid the need for constituency representation. Constituencies of 500,000 or so electors! Do they, can they, have any real contact with or knowledge of their MEPs? Meanwhile parties with substantial electoral support are denied any representation and that cannot be just.

Regrettably, on virtually all these significant constitutional issues Britain rejects reform.

Fifthly, one must not overlook the *Economic and Social Committee* (bearing the elegant acronym 'ECOSOC'). It is perhaps the least known of the Community institutions and yet enjoys a consultative role not far removed from that of the European Parliament. Comprised of members appointed by the national governments and representing groups of employers, trade unions and miscellaneous interests, ECOSOC constitutes another element in the Community's decision-making process and has to be consulted by both the Commission and the Council before new laws are passed. However, it has no powers to impose its views and herein lies one of its weaknesses.

Another inherent problem is the manner of selection which relies on lists submitted to and selected by national governments, with the inevitable political overtones. This means that the composition of ECOSOC may fail to reflect the true political complexion of the member state, further reinforcing the arguments of those who see the committee as both unrepresentative and undemocratic. Reform might be possible in the shape of more transparent procedures for selection, or in the more radical proposal for reconstituting ECOSOC as a second tier of a reformed European Parliament. Whatever approach is adopted, the present situation is inappropriate for the 1990s.

Outside the formal structures of Parliament and ECOSOC, special interest groups will doubtless remain active during the coming decade. Of greater importance, however, is that ordinary citizens grasp the available opportunities for being more active. Industrialists can do this by offering themselves as members of technical committees responsible for defining new European standards. At present many such committees are dominated by mainland Europeans and the Department of Trade and Industry and others have urged British technicians to become more active. If they do not, then they have only themselves to blame if British standards and ideas do not prevail.

In the field of social policy, British trade unions are active in Europe but frequently lack or are unwilling to commit the resources and man-power on the same level as their counterparts in France or Germany. The same is true of consumer groups and environmental groups, who are perenially under-staffed and under-funded. As citizens of Europe, we should all be more vociferous and more actively involved.

WIDER ISSUES

Coming to the broader issues, there is clearly a case for wider integration of European policies in transport, freedom of movement of people and co-ordination of environmental standards. Britain's transport infrastructure is grossly inferior to that of much of the rest of Europe and certainly that of the northern countries. There are serious question marks over the viability of the Channel Tunnel as a result of the doctrinaire insistence on private funding and little short of a miracle will ensure its opening on time in 1993. And even if and when it is functioning, while Europe is busy developing its complementary, supporting road and rail networks, the routes to London remain stuck at a planning stage, with vital extensions to the west of Scotland and Wales, the North East, the North-West and Scotland no more than twinkles in the planners' eyes – to the frustration of provincial businesses which are, at the same time, being urged to take advantage of the single market. And what sense does it make for air traffic control to be so diffuse and for progress to greater integration to be thwarted by the irrelevant arguments about sovereignty?

Resistance to the development of a Community infrastructure policy, of a high-speed rail network, of more advanced combined road–rail transport and, indeed, of giving greater emphasis to the complementarity of the different modes of transport combine to demonstrate yet again the insular, myopic and self-defeating approach of Britain towards the EC and even the single market, in which the government professes such belief, for surely it should be self-evident that it can only function if people and goods can be transported across frontiers far more efficiently than at present. Can we be satisfied, despite all the advertising gloss, that Britain is determined to adopt the precept that environmental considerations must be central to all areas of policy-making as laid down in the SEA and the Community's Fourth Environment Action Programme? How profound is our commitment to the concept of 'sustainable development' which goes to the very root of global environmental policy?

Will there be eventual monetary union and progress on the Delors proposals? I have to say that Britain's oft-stated assertion that we would join the Exchange Rate Mechanism of the European Monetary System 'when the time is ripe' produced only weary derision from our partners. And the government's weasel words concerning the questions of a central bank and a common currency produce scepticism about our very concept of what the European Community should be about.

To stand by on the touchline while this game proceeds is to run the risk of being marginalised when the decisions come to be made – and made they almost certainly will be, with or without Britain's participation. Here, as in other areas, the 1990s may see Europe advancing at two speeds with Britain holding back in the slow lane. The risks to Britain as a financial centre are all too clear.

A NEW – AND ENLARGED – EUROPE?

As dramatic headlines continue to emerge from the burgeoning democracies of Eastern Europe, a huge step towards European economic integration is taking place virtually unnoticed. Work is proceeding between the European Community and EFTA countries to establish an expanded free trade association and customs union. The merging of the two is unlikely but closer co-operation is inevitable. This has been made clear by the decision spearheaded by President Delors based essentially on the anxieties of the poorer EC countries that EFTA is deriving advantages of Community membership at their, the poorer nations', expense. Thus the Commission has taken the interim step, allowing the EFTA countries a role in shaping decisions but at the same time denying them a place at the table where decisions are made.

So what is to be the shape of the Community after 1992? How much national sovereignty will have to be yielded to achieve a common purpose in international relations? Will frontiers have to be abandoned and if so to what extent? How much more fiscal and monetary sovereignty will have to be surrendered? Of course, many of these areas of sovereignty have already been substantially eroded and the development of the 'New Europe' towards greater integration – political, economic and security – is inexorable.

Rather than treat the convulsive events in Eastern Europe as a pretext for slowing down the whole European operation (except, of course, for those bits and pieces that Britain likes!), as recommended by Mrs Thatcher, Jacques Delors – backed by the overwhelming majority of the member states and the European Parliament – has urged that the construction of the 'New Europe' must move ahead.

I am reminded in this context of the two politicians – one British, one French – who went on safari together. They found themselves cut off from their party in the African bush. A none-too-friendly lion approached. Whereupon the Frenchman reached for his bag and started putting on his running shoes.

'You'll never run faster than the lion,' said the Englishman.

'That doesn't matter,' said the Frenchman, 'as long as I can run faster than you.'

The moral of the story requires no further underlining. I believe passionately that this is certainly no time to pause. As far as EFTA is concerned, some members may opt to become part of the Community and help, therefore, to make its decisions. Others, however, may wish to remain outside. But whatever happens, the new relationship will take the form of a full free-trade association and customs agreement, with the abolition of tariffs and quotas, with the harmonisation of product standards, with the EFTA countries moving towards the Community's position on matters such as public procurement and telecommunications. In other words, the EFTA countries will take upon themselves, prior to some of them joining the EC, certain parts of the Treaty of Rome and inevitably they will be forced to parallel, if not participate in, the agricultural reform programme of the EC, and perhaps accompany the EC as it moves in the direction of economic and monetary union.

What then of Eastern Europe? What I believe the peoples of Hungary, Poland, Czechoslovakia and others want is not a European Community weakened by stalling progress, incapable therefore of mounting an economic challenge to the United States of America and Japan. Ultimately, they would wish to see themselves as being associated with an economically strong Europe and unmistakably, therefore, their message is 'get on with your integration'.

In the shorter term, the rise of democracy in Eastern Europe represents a major challenge to the Community as an enormous market for both goods and services is opened up, coupled with a pool of cheap labour. The Community will have to promote a firm and effective policy of extending its European ideals of equality, freedom and social justice to the newly emerging Eastern states, in order to prevent their becoming simply extended markets or sources of low-cost labour. The environmental challenge is also huge and one in which the industrially advanced nations of the Community, despite the fact that they are not without blemishes themselves, can bring economic, technical and specialist aid to the ravaged environments of Eastern Europe.

Equality, freedom, social justice and the environment are the same elements that should apply to the Community's relationships to the less-developed countries. While there is considerable talk about the opportunities that the single market will provide, particularly for the African, Caribbean and Pacific (ACP) countries who are signatories to the Lomé Convention (which guarantees a European market for many of their products), the reality is that the export of manufactured goods by the ACP states to the Community, the USA and Japan has fallen by more than half since 1970. Exports of capital goods to many of the ACP states by the developed countries are also falling, leading to fears that these countries may find themselves ill-prepared to take advantage of the opportunities of the next decade. Already the ACP states are being encouraged to develop 'regional markets' along the lines of the European Communities, but there are real fears that an impregnable European fortress may be attempting to close its doors on them. It will require vision and statesmanship to resolve the issue of the Community's future relationships with the Third World.

A FEDERAL EUROPE?

A federal Europe? Who knows? But how far and how fast we use the means provided in the Single European Act to draw closer together in the spheres of industrial, transport, technological, social, monetary and political philosophies must depend on the men and women of vision, and perhaps too on the young people in the member states who over the next decade will become the first true Europeans. They will be helped by increased opportunities for exchanges, visits and learning languages. But for us in Britain so much needs to change.

There is also a dimension to the arguments about the internal market and economic integration which, though prevalent in Europe, is almost completely missing in Britain. For many in Europe integration was – and remains – a *political* objective, and this includes those on the left for whom the concept of a United Europe is in itself a socialist policy. The cultural, historical and social origins of the passion for Europe, which is reflected in so many political parties on the Continent, including the left, have moulded these ideas. What we should certainly note is that for many European political parties, the political arguments about the value of integration certainly take precedence over the economic arguments. This is a crucial difference in perspective which we in Britain must try to understand better as we advance towards and look beyond 1992. After all, if one believes the internal market is the mortar of political union, then one may well have a view of the process which is totally different from the view of someone who is cool or even hostile to the very idea of union. Regrettably, these concepts seem very distant from the extraordinarily purblind view towards Europe so often expressed by Mrs Thatcher – usually after she had just signed some important Community declaration.

I have, however, been encouraged by the developments in what was East Germany, by the evident desire to accept the thesis of the European Commission that the only way to forge a Community is to blend the advantages of a market economy with the regulation and the social vision to protect and enhance the quality of life of our citizens and, indeed, those countless millions beyond. That philosophy is anathematic to Mrs Thatcher. It is this division that brought her all the way from London to Bruges.

Perhaps the prospects for the future can best be summed up by my former Commission colleague, Claude Cheysson, when he said: 'My dream of Europe is Mrs Thatcher's nightmare.' Mrs Thatcher has now departed Downing Street. Whether her nightmare is shared fully by her successor remains to be seen.

NOTES

1. It is ironic that the concept of a new-style Marshall Plan is being revived in the wake of the extraordinary events which have so recently occurred in Eastern Europe.
2. Lord Cockfield was the senior Commissioner for the UK with responsibility *inter alia* for the internal market from 1985 to 1989.

7. Parliamentary Sovereignty in the 1990s

J. Enoch Powell

Let me offer my definition of parliamentary sovereignty by saying that, if the United Kingdom has parliamentary sovereignty, the laws of the United Kingdom are made by or by the authority of Parliament, the taxes are levied by the authority of the House of Commons and, in consequence of those two powers, the government and its policies are subject to the approval of Parliament. There is a certain haziness as to whether by Parliament one means, as one correctly should, Queen, Lords and Commons, or whether one is, as Viscount Tonypandy is liable to do, talking in fact about the House of Commons when one uses the expression Parliament. So I am talking about a country of which the government effectively is vested in and controlled by a Parliament of which the effective controlling element is the House of Commons, and this means that the sovereignty in an ultimate and perhaps metaphorical sense is exercised by the electorate which remakes at periodic intervals that House of Commons.

I have divided my discourse into three sections. The first is to relate what happened since 1970, the second is why, and the third is what will happen in the 1990s. Now I must warn you that I am a bad witness in all these compartments. I am a bad witness on what happened and why, because I myself was passionately involved in the struggle against Britain's membership of the European Economic Community. Indeed, it was my opposition to that which severed me from the Conservative Party and dominated the last 15 to 20 years of my political existence. I am therefore emotionally as well as intellectually and academically interested in what happened and my analysis of why it happened partakes of the partisan. As regards what will happen in the 1990s, we have had no end of a lesson in the recent past. We have been reminded in recent years in dramatic manner that we cannot foresee the future. It is one of the most important lessons which the working politician learns, that he must not behave as if he could foresee the future and that his notions of the future should be very severely policed, if he intends to act upon them, by the realisation that he is almost certain to be wrong in his anticipation. There are however certain antidotes to our inability to foresee the future, and to those I will come when I approach that section of my task.

What has happened since 1970? Well, the most important thing that has happened since 1970 is that in 1972 Parliament, including the House of Commons specifically, in the most comprehensive manner by statute destroyed the parliamentary sovereignty of the United Kingdom by vesting the overriding power of legislation, the overriding power of jurisdiction and the overriding power of taxation in an external body. This was not something which I personally believed the House of Commons would or could ever do. So 1972 was not only a shattering year in my own life but it was a year in which I became aware that my assumptions as to what the people of this country would tolerate, what they would allow to be done to them, had been too narrow. In the years since 1970 until quite recently their docility, which is quite a marked characteristic – 'deference' was Bagehot's word for it, and a very good word too – which makes them governable, if not parliamentarily governable, has been exemplified by their indifference to the practical effects of the surrender which was enacted in 1972.

That was followed by the introduction in 1978 of direct elections to a European representative body. Now the significance of that in relation to parliamentary sovereignty is that the elected body – though it is not elected in accordance with the Treaty of Rome or Brussels, which requires that it should be elected by proportional representation – is a body in which automatically and of necessity the representatives of the United Kingdom are in a permanent minority. So the electorate of the United Kingdom did not refuse to elect representatives to an assembly in which the representatives of the United Kingdom would be in a permanent minority. It was, it is true, an assembly with relatively few effective powers but, as I argued when opposing the passing of the enabling act, its power to dismiss the Commission is quite an important power and can be successfully exploited, as indeed can its power to pass the budget. I told my fellow countrymen, who took no notice, that it was from powers such as these that their own control over legislation, taxation and the executive had evolved over five centuries and therefore they should not be indifferent to those powers being exercised by a body, purporting to represent them, amongst others, which possessed those powers and which like all such bodies presently proved itself to be greedy of the consequences of possessing them. Elect a representative assembly and it will be greedy to exploit the implications of representation. It was an important step, in that it transferred to those elected by a number of different electorates put together the characteristics which in the United Kingdom had hitherto been associated with the electorate of the United Kingdom itself. It was thus a denial of the necessary homogeneity of an electorate upon which some of the prime characteristics of the Parliament of the United Kingdom have been based.

Partly as a consequence of that extension of the effective powers of the authority to which Parliament had renounced its sovereignty in the United Kingdom, the Single European Act, implemented by amendment of the 1972 Act in 1986, greatly restricted the powers of the representative of the United Kingdom in the Council of Ministers, by subordinating not merely questions of a trading nature but questions, however broad, which might be adjudged by the European Court to be implicit in the European 'single market' to the rule of the majority vote. Thereby one of the safeguards which had been held out to the people of this country in the early 1970s, namely that they would continue to control the United Kingdom government's input to the new external authority, was for practical purposes swept away – for practical purposes, since the European Court does not interpret the law in the sense in which the courts of the United Kingdom interpret law, but is in the full continental sense a law-inventing authority which rules upon general principles and general presumptions. Thus no definition referrable to the European Court can be relied upon to limit the exercise of authority by the external authority empowered in 1972.

All that happened in the last 20 years; and it happened until recently with the comparative apparent indifference of the people of this country who, when they were told at elections, 'You are electing people who are not going to control the legislation which governs your behaviour in the United Kingdom, who are not going to be the sole judges of how you should be taxed, who are not going to control the policy by which the United Kingdom's government is actuated', took remarkably little interest.

There has however in the last two or three years been an important change in that respect, and the implications of what was done in 1972, '78 and '86 have begun to be topics of allowable conversation in decent circles in political quarters. This could not have happened if there had not been a change in the electoral perception. When the then Prime Minister of the

United Kingdom, not without support from certain quarters in the British Foreign Office, took the step of frontally attacking the implications of membership of the European Economic Community, as defined by the Act of 1972, in her speech at Bruges in September 1988, she would scarcely have done so unless she supposed that this was a topic which had at last become ripe for public ventilation and of which the public ventilation was likely to bring advantage – electoral advantage – to those who ventilated it. So there has been a change in that which can be stated without discredit or ridicule. There has been a change, in that it has become possible in the last two years to argue the case, at least, that the people of the United Kingdom ought only to be governed by laws which are made by their Parliament, and ought only to pay taxes which are levied by their House of Commons, ought only to be called upon to comply with policies for which their government is responsible to Parliament. There has been a change in the atmosphere. That change in the atmosphere, like so many good things, could be viewed as having come from the East. The analysis which I will presently offer of the reasons will indicate why events in Eastern and Central Europe have contributed mightily to that changed atmosphere, to a virtual reversion to the attitude which I had fondly assumed would have been present and available in and after 1972.

So I address myself at once to the reasons why I was mistaken; and I invite you to note and to admire the phenomenon of a politician explaining to you, or endeavouring to explain why he was mistaken. After all, I did venture on one occasion when I was in Russia interviewing some of the spokesmen of the Russian administration to take the liberty of joking with the Russians to say: 'You know we have a proverb in Britain?' 'Oh, and what is that?' 'Enoch was right'. This was not taken as seriously as I had intended it to be taken; but at any rate here is the subject of that British proverb analysing for you the reasons why he was wrong in 1972.

The first reason which I identify is that I had underestimated the post-imperial trauma of my fellow countrymen. Perhaps I should apologise for that trauma as a Birmingham man since the British Empire, as envisaged by Joseph Chamberlain, had a lot to do with Britain's post-imperial trauma in the years after 1945. I was born in 1912 and therefore as a child lived in a country whose young generation was thrilled to glory in the immense size of the state to which they belonged. It was a big nation, a big show to which one belonged by virtue of belonging to the United Kingdom. Britain – the short little title for the United Kingdom of Great Britain and Northern Island, but previously Great Britain and Ireland – was great because Britain was big and it was self-evidently big as any map would verify. Now after 1945, partly because of the American factor but also partly because of visible and inevitable contraction, that Britain to which people belonged ceased to be big. So the deduction was drawn : 'We are no longer big and we are no longer going to be big. Therefore we shall be unimportant, and the cure is to get in on something big.' In the debates of the early 1970s the bullfrog motivation was very clear on the Conservative side of the House, and it was after all the Conservative side of the House which, albeit only by eight votes, carried the European Communities Bill of 1972. We were great, we want to remain great, we must therefore belong to something big; and talking in the insufferable way that the English sometimes will talk they proceeded to say: 'And we must therefore lead in Europe.' Now the notion of those who inhabit an offshore island 'leading' those who inhabit the continent is so ridiculous that the absurdity of it hardly needs to be mentioned; but the very absurdity underlines my belief that post-imperial trauma was one of the reasons why the people of the United Kingdom remained passive when their sovereignty, exercised through Parliament, was taken away from them, and taken away from them with a certain ringing of bells.

I mentioned the United States. The propaganda of the closing years of the Second World War had inculcated into the British the notion that the Americans had won the war. This is not true. They themselves – the British – had won the war in 1940; they had proved themselves invincible in 1940 as in 1805 and 1588. But the whole atmosphere in which under a Prime Minister who had an American mother (a fact about Churchill never to be forgotten) we had been an apparently junior ally of the United States made them easy victims to the belief that they had been dependent for survival, for victory, upon the United States. It followed that they would remain dependent for safety against a continental enemy, a future continental empire, upon the same source of strength and assistance.

This delusion of being dependent for safety and protection upon the goodwill of the United States was multiplied when the nuclear deterrent was invented in the 1950s. The theory of the nuclear deterrent asserted that you enjoy safety and peace because of the willingness of the people of the United States to commit nuclear suicide rather than that there should be a disturbance of the balance of power in Europe. It never was credible, it never made the slightest degree of sense that they would behave in such a way, least of all on that account, but it was so convenient an hypothesis that for 30 years successive United Kingdom governments lived upon it and conducted the defence of the realm upon it. The beauty of it was that of course it is exceedingly cheap; if within two or five days of the commencement of hostilities everything is to be blown to smithereens, your defence preparations can be relatively modest and the invitation to match the large defence preparations of other countries can be readily resisted. The United Kingdom swallowed the hook, the line and the sinker when it was abolishing National Service prospectively in 1957. I should know because I was Financial Secretary to the Treasury in that year. I know, therefore, that the consequent financial gain to the Ministry of Defence from embracing the nuclear deterrent as the basis of British defence policy was enormous. There never really was any reason for the United Kingdom to have conscription, but that case was unnecessary to argue if it was over-trumped by the nuclear deterrent as the self-evident guarantee of British integrity and safety.

We experienced in 1956 an event – the Suez invasion – which confirmed us in our conviction that it is an axiom that the policy of the United Kingdom cannot seriously diverge from the wishes of the United States since the United States is, for practical purposes, all-powerful. The assumed omnipotence of the United States was embraced, greedily embraced, by Harold Macmillan at the end of 1956 though he was, in fact, only deducing it from another fallacy; the supposed necessity of a fixed exchange rate for the pound sterling in terms of the dollar. But Suez inaugurated a period of 30 years of British foreign policy in which an axiom held unchallenged sway – 'If the Yanks want it, give it to them'. However the Yanks saw Europe, however they saw the United Kingdom, however they saw the world, we had to conform to that vision, to that philosophy and whatever deductions the United States drew from it.

Now, the United States is inhabited by people who are very slow to recognise that the rest of the world is inhabited by people different than themselves. They have an inbuilt inability to accept the existence of foreigners from which we in this country do not suffer: after all, we know that we are British and all the others are foreigners. This gives us a very valuable interest in looking at foreigners, examining those strange beings and wondering and studying what it is that motivates them. The Americans are not troubled in such ways because they know that the rest of mankind was destined to be free as they are free and was endowed too by the Almighty, though His intentions have been unhappily frustrated, with the same opportunities as the people of the United States. The result is that they survey Europe with the same long-range telescopes as they use for surveying the moon and more distant planets. Looking at Europe with such optics they said: 'My God, there's a lot of little countries there.

That's terrible. How can we possibly promise to commit suicide when they're all split up into a lot of little countries? You never know what they'll be doing next.'

Then was invented the portentous metaphor of the 'European Pillar' which was to correspond to the American Pillar of the Grand Alliance, the overarching defence of human freedom constituted by the Americans' presumed suicidal intention. The Americans were therefore looking for something on this side of their trip line which would be sufficiently reliable – or perhaps I should say sufficiently intelligible – to render their suicide pact less incredible. This led them to the deduction that those little countries all ought to be unified, they ought to be brought together into one mass, into one political entity – like the United States, which in its wisdom comprises some 50 states.

So the desirability of a United States of Western Europe was one of the riders deduced from the axiom of the nuclear deterrent, and hence one of the riders attached to the presumed axiom dictating British defence and foreign policy. 'We want you British to get in there with the rest of them and help make a unified mass so that we will have a single policy in Europe and make some sense of our commitment to Europe.'

That was undoubtedly one of the factors which operated upon the United Kingdom at a departmental and ministerial level and communicated the final push into joining the European Economic Community. America was behind it and the supposed imperatives of our alliance with America. There was another related cause at work: we got used – since we invented 'the world' in the course of the Second World War – to having a world. Now the important thing about the world is that for political purposes there is no such place. It is a marvellous statistical construct. A race of men exists who spend their time compiling economic statistics; and no power on earth can prevent them from putting those statistics together, sticking the word 'world' in front of them and declaring that they are telling us about world trade, world population or world production. It is a notion closely associated with the Great American Delusion. It is a state of mind in which we have been content to live since the Second World War – it made it so much more comfortable for getting on with the Americans and it made it so much easier finding brick-bats which politicians could throw at one another. There's nothing like an international league table for providing silly brick-bats for throwing at other silly people.

Now these statistics were most alarming. In the 1960s and 1970s they were showing that the population of the world was outgrowing its resources; a very disagreeable prospect, since there would be all kinds of shortages; above all there would be shortages of food. In 1972 the people of this country were warned that unless they joined the European Economic Community they would starve, that they would be dependent upon the growth of food in Europe in which they must secure a share. The notion of a starving world provided the fuel for a debate which was fought – and some of us thought was won – at the end of the 1970s between the monetarists and their opponents. Their opponents are the dirigistes who believe that economies are there to be directed, while monetarists believe you can leave them alone and they will generally behave more sensibly than any politician. The European Economic Community was purpose-built for the dirigistes if only because its bureaucracy depended for occupation upon economic constructs. So there was the affinity between the barely defeated force which monetarism had opposed and the European Economic Community. It was home territory to the dirigistes, it was the grand citadel of the managers of economies. The deduction was drawn from this that as you are going to be managed anyhow, you had better get together with those who are going to manage you. The CBI can be heard talking this sort of bilge to this very day: you are going to be managed anyhow, your exchange rate is going to be managed anyhow, your economy is going to be managed anyhow: so better, since it is going to be managed anyhow, be one of the manipulators even if you are only in a minority amongst them.

Such are what I can discern at varying levels as the explanations why the people of this country were induced to sell their 'eternal jewel' of parliamentary self-government, a jewel which other countries are now greedily grasping in order to become part of a European Economic Community now in a state of advanced disarray. If the role of the United States as the indispensable defender of the United Kingdom and its allies against the oncoming Russian hordes was ever credible, it is no longer credible – so incredible that the Americans themselves find it incredible and are folding up their tents and softly and silently vanishing away. But if the Americans are going, there's much less fun and much less motivation than there used to be in sustaining structures wished upon you by the United States and in conforming with an American view of the European continent. If the United States, which found it comfortable and convenient to have a single political entity constructed in Western Europe, is no longer indispensable for your national purposes, perhaps after all it was not indispensable to abandon your own self-government in order to be part of that entity.

There has also been the psychological impact of the discovery that there are still such things as nations, nations in the sense of groups of people who wish to govern themselves and not be governed from outside. Of course this was highly laudable when those outside were in the Kremlin; but the idea began to dawn: 'If it is good for the Hungarians to govern themselves, why is it bad for the British to govern themselves? If the Hungarians hope to get on without being governed from outside, why does the United Kingdom have to pool its self-government in a larger entity in Western Europe?' Furthermore, not unforeseen by the present deponent as far back as 1971 when opposing entry into the European Economic Community, there was the grand factor of Germany, a reunited Germany, which arrived upon the scene. Now West Germany had done very well out of membership of the European Economic Community. They didn't have to give up anything because they had no historical self-government to give up; they had no parliamentary sovereignty – that was wished upon them by their victors. They had nothing to give up. But in return for nothing they got respect and respectability, as well as huge trading opportunities. However, if to form part of a block with the other nations of Western Europe were an obstacle to their becoming Gross Deutschland again, they would prefer being Gross Deutschland to remaining part of a West European block.

This has always been predictable, except that it was so uncomfortable to predict it and it looked so improbable until quite recently that it was not taken seriously. However, the mechanics have been working their way out under one's eyes almost day by day. So it was not surprising that in the last two or three years it has been possible once again to use the word 'nation' which used to be greeted with hollow laughter, and to use the word 'sovereign' otherwise than ironically, and it was possible for the then Prime Minister, who maybe had underestimated the continuing potency of the factors which I have identified, to see political advantage in reasserting the right of the United Kingdom to manage its own affairs, though admittedly under circumstances of freedom of trade and intercourse with the adjacent nations of Western Europe.

I have now done parts one and two of the question but am left with the most perilous, the 1990s, about which I know nothing whatsoever. So what are my guides in the darkness which lies ahead? The politician is in the same situation as Virgil in Dante's *Divine Comedy*, who carries the lantern behind him, throwing light to those that come behind him while he himself walks in darkness. The historian, the political scientist and the politician – whether or not they shed much light behind – themselves walk in darkness, but they have to have some encouragement for walking in darkness, and I am going to share with you my own particular personal encouragement. I've stolen it, as one often does steal a handy metaphor, from other disciplines. I deeply believe in the tendency to 'revert to type'; I do believe there is such a thing as a society (unlike Margaret Thatcher apparently); I do also believe that a society is a quasi-biological entity and I believe that societies are quasi-biological entities which tend to revert to type. The belief has encouraged me through all these last dreary nigh 20 years.

My fellow-countrymen, it is true, have not bestirred themselves to defend or to regain the 'eternal jewel' which distinguished them in their own eyes, until recently, from all the other nations upon Earth; but it is not in their nature once they are conscious of it to allow themselves to be deprived of it. I use the theory of reversion to type as my guide to what is going to happen in the 1990s or maybe to what I shall discover has not happened in the 1990s. I am waiting, though with more expectancy than certainty, for the people of the United Kingdom, or more correctly speaking the English (for they created parliamentary sovereignty because they created Parliament), to revert to type. Of course, they may revert to type too late; but then it's another of their national characteristics that they become aware of loss and danger and deprivation when everyone else thought that they had irrevocably lost. Take no notice therefore of continentals. Take no notice of *Homo europeus* who tells you : 'The Brits can't get out now.' The Brits can always get out if they want to, and if they revert to type they will want to, and their desire to do so will be catered for by those who desire power and the other emoluments which depend upon their votes. But they will be assisted in that reversion by the fact that, both in respect of Europe and in respect of the United States, we are at present only in the very early stages of a process. What has happened in 1989 and 1990 in Eastern Europe is the beginning of a reversion – and I am going to use the term again – to an older Europe, the Europe of Metternich, the Europe of 1815.

Now 1815 was an interesting year, and how glad I was to see Sir Michael Howard in 1989 referring once again in *The Times* to 1815 as the year which was coming back. 1815 was a grand year, the year of the Congress of Vienna. The seats they sat on may be seen at Mount Stewart by visitors to Northern Ireland if they care to visit the house which didn't ever belong to Viscount Castlereagh. Still, he got the chairs from the Congress of Vienna and there they are with the arms of all the countries represented on the backs. But that is a digression, as you will readily recognise. So back to 1815 and the Congress of Vienna. We haven't yet had a peace after the Second World War and perhaps that's lucky because otherwise we might have had a Versailles or we might have had an American peace. As it is we shall have a European peace. Peace in 1815 was shaped under the influence of two powers – the two European powers which had proved invincible: Russia and Britain, the Tsar Alexander and Viscount Castlereagh, but they had assistance. They had assistance from two very wise men in the Abbé Tallyrand (who knew a lot about the French, France and Europe) and Prince Metternich (who knew a great deal about Central and Eastern Europe) and between them they made a pretty good job of it until it was all upset at the Battle of Koniggrätz in 1866.

We are reverting. Europe is reverting, as the nations which comprise it emerge from under the nuclear ice, to its old self. They're discovering their old selves – it is their old, not new selves that they are discovering. Yugoslavia did not go to the congress at Budapest recently in order to discover Yugoslavia. It went to discover the Holy Roman Empire; the British Foreign Office also has rediscovered the Holy Roman Empire. They are rediscovering their past selves and that process is only in its earliest stages: it is due to grow and to expand and to fructify. The withdrawal of the United States from a continent to which it does not belong, a continent which it does not understand and a continent for whose internal arrangements its interference is no longer required, is also in the early stages. So I expect to see the development in the 1990s of those two trends; the reversion of Europe to the Europe of 1815 and the withdrawal of the United States, which will also be a reversion to type, to what the United States was intended to be – an isolationist country on the other side of a very broad ocean.

One thing I didn't understand about the Americans when I first met them (and that's not so long ago), was what they were afraid of. They seemed to be terribly frightened and I said : 'What is it that you are frightened of? We are only 21 miles away from the blighters. What have *you* got to be frightened of?' They didn't answer me; but very often you find out the answer from people who won't answer you; it's what they say when they're trying not to answer, when they're sorting themselves out in the attempt to avoid some sort of answer. What they were afraid of was having nobody else to talk to, a world in which they would be alone. Well, a world in which they have made themselves alone is the world to which the United States is destined forever if it reverts to type.

So, I look ahead with some hopefulness, but I must caution you against an old man who hopes. I have made in recent months an important psychological discovery. I call it the Moses Syndrome. There was Moses on the east bank of Jordan, and I know just what it was like; he was too old and he'd been told on the highest authority, 'You're not going into the promised land.' So he sat there and he thought he saw it and he thought he foresaw the arrangements which would be made there. I call that the Moses Syndrome. Old people who have been thrown on the scrap-heap, particularly the scrap-heap of politics, are particularly vulnerable to the Moses Syndrome, to thinking that at last, just in time before they die, they are seeing the causes for which they have immolated themselves about to be achieved. So I end as I began, as I properly should in any academic environment, with a health warning.

8.   In Defence of the Constitution: A Riposte to the Radicals

Philip Norton

In the 1950s the British Constitution was – as we saw in Chapter 1 – taken largely for granted. The country was enjoying relative economic prosperity. The institutions of government appeared able to deliver the goods expected of them. The political system was praised for producing coherent policy outcomes rather than political stalemate. The Westminster model of government was considered exportable to newly independent states. Writers in a number of other countries, including the United States, also sought to draw on that model in order to improve the effectiveness of their own political systems.[1]

The picture has changed over the past 30 years. Economic downturn (inflation, unemployment, recession and relative economic decline) coupled with political turmoil and uncertainty (the 'troubles' in Northern Ireland, an indeterminate general election outcome in 1974, a relative decline in support for the two principal parties, a growing political bifurcation between north and south) have encouraged a questioning of the political system itself. The rules and customs that form 'the Constitution' have been seen by some commentators to be dysfunctional. They have ceased to produce the goods expected of them. Consequently, calls have variously been made for radical constitutional reform, including a new 'constitutional settlement'.

However, to identify such upheaval – political and economic – as generating pressure for change is to identify only part of the reason for the upsurge in demand for reform of the Constitution. It is a necessary but not a sufficient condition. To the developments already identified must be added political judgement. Changes in the constitution have often taken the form of measures deemed politically expedient. Politicians responsible for reform have proceeded not on the basis of first principles but on a calculation of political advantage. (Reform has been opposed on the same basis.) Major changes are variously made by governments in order to remove obstacles to the achievement of policy goals (limiting the powers of the House of Lords, abolishing the Greater London Council) or are advocated by the 'outs' in politics as a means either of restricting the powers of the existing regime or of facilitating their own return to office.

Much, indeed most, of the running in the present debate has been made by the 'outs' in politics. Advocacy of a new Constitution has largely been the prerogative of the politically dispossessed. The Liberals (now part of the Liberal Democratic Party) are longstanding advocates of radical constitutional change. In the latter half of the 1970s their numbers were swelled by many on the right, fearful of the effects of a Labour government returned to office on the votes of less than 40 per cent of those who went to the polling booths. Lord Hailsham discerned the dangers of an 'elective dictatorship' and proposed both a new Bill of Rights and a written Constitution.[2] Sir Keith Joseph argued that a Bill of Rights should place 'a constitutional limit on taxation, that is taxation on incomes and property, during life and death'.[3] Some Conservatives who had previously been defenders of the existing electoral system began to appreciate the value of a new system. A system based on proportional representation (PR) was seen as a means of preventing single-party extremism in government. Conservative Action for Electoral Reform (CAER) came into being. The volume *Adversary Politics and Electoral Reform*, edited by S. E. Finer (and published in 1975 by the founder of CAER, Anthony Wigram), had a seminal influence. By the late 1970s pressure for constitutional change was marked among the ranks of the centre and right in British politics; support for a Bill of Rights was especially pronounced in the House of Lords, backed by a coalition of Conservative, Liberal and cross-bench jurists.

The return of a Conservative government in 1979 took much of the wind out of the reformist sails of many on the right. Those who were now the 'ins' in politics – such as Hailsham and Joseph – were silenced. The 'outs' of the centre and those on the right (the 'wets') continued to press for change, but their calls were largely drowned out in a new era of majority government. However, as the 1980s progressed, those calling for a new constitutional settlement began to swell in number and support for change took on a new political configuration.

Reform of the Constitution became increasingly attractive to many on the left, especially in the wake of the third consecutive election victory for the Conservatives in 1987. The plurality first-past-the-post system of electing MPs was seen as no longer benefiting the two largest parties (receiving a greater proportion of seats than votes cast and offering the likelihood of an overall parliamentary majority) but as benefiting one party in particular – the Conservative Party – with Labour being in danger of assuming the position of a second party that was a permanent 'out' party. This view was reinforced by the redrawing of the constituency boundaries in 1982 and fuelled by the expectations of the boundary review due in the mid 1990s – a population shift from urban to rural areas favouring the Conservative cause. Reinforced by perceptions of a government bent on centralising power, systemic change began to be looked at in a new light.

Support for constitutional reform has thus shifted in recent years. It has found supporters on the Labour front bench, Shadow Cabinet member Robin Cook in particular arguing the case for proportional representation. The Labour Campaign for Electoral Reform, which lost virtually all its parliamentary support when the Social Democratic Party was formed in 1981 (leaving Austin Mitchell as a forlorn exponent of PR on the Labour benches), has garnered new support. Labour MP Jeff Rooker claims to have obtained the signatures of 40 Labour colleagues in a private survey he conducted in 1990 on the merits of changing the voting system.[4]

Support for wider constitutional change has found expression through the medium of Charter '88. This comprises 'an informal association of individuals and bodies, including the *New Statesman* and the Constitutional Reform Centre' and was brought into being in the tercentenary year of the Glorious Revolution. Contending that absolute power is in the hands of a 'parliamentary oligarchy', the Charter proposes a Bill of Rights, electoral reform (with the introduction of a system of PR), a reformed non-hereditary Upper House, freedom of information, executive powers subject to the rule of law, reform of the judiciary, 'a democratically renewed Parliament', and equitable distribution of power between different tiers of government, all these provisions to be embodied in a written Constitution.

When first published, the Charter attracted the support of the evergreen reformers of the centre (Lord Bonham-Carter, Lord Jenkins of Hillhead, Ludovic Kennedy, David Marquand, Baroness Seear and Des Wilson being among the more prominent) as well as – more significantly – an array of intellectuals and political activists on the left. Among the more prominent of this latter group were Anthony Arblaster, Bernard Crick, Stuart Hall, Martin Jacques (editor of *Marxism Today*), Bruce Kent (of CND), Steven Lukes, Ralph Miliband, Tom Nairn and Bhikhu Parekh. More, including Peter Tatchell (the Labour activist once denounced by Michael Foot when party leader), later added their names. By the summer of 1990, the Charter was claiming at least 20,000 signatories.

Support for constitutional reform – either particular reforms or a wholescale reformulation of the existing Constitution – thus spans a broader political spectrum than was the case in previous decades. It encompasses the political centre, elements of the centre-right (the 'wet' tendency of the Conservative Party in particular, though by no means confined to that tendency[5]) and disparate but growing elements on the left, including a number of Marxists. This growing band has made, and continues to make, most of the running in debate. As we shall see, literature seeking to identify the faults of the present system – particularly the encroachment by government on civil liberties – is burgeoning. Few works have appeared that have challenged it.

Indeed, support for a new constitutional settlement appears to have attained the status of a fashion, especially among the chattering classes: those intellectuals and artists prone to make public appearances and pronouncements. This is exemplified by many of the signatures carried by Charter '88. In part, the list reads like a roll-call of the great and good among the literary, artistic and even clerical world. It includes novelists and playwrights Martin Amis, Alan Bleasdale, Margaret Drabble, Lady Antonia Fraser, David Lodge, Harold Pinter, Alan Plater and Salman Rushdie; thespians Dame Peggy Ashcroft, Simon Callow, John Cleese, Julie Christie, Dame Judi Dench and Glenda Jackson; film makers Derek Jarman and David Putnam; musician Simon Rattle; clerics the Bishops of Oxford (Richard Harries) and Birmingham (Mark Santer); and television personalities ranging from Melvyn Bragg and Bamber Gascoigne to 'agony aunt' Claire Rayner.

Among intellectuals not persuaded by the Charter, few appear willing to challenge publicly and in print the views expressed by such a glittering array. It is a situation that the Third Marquess of Salisbury would have understood and of which he would have despaired. As a Tory pessimist, he accepted on occasion measures that he disapproved of but which he deemed to be the fashion of the day, 'and against fashion it is almost impossible to argue'.[6] This chapter proposes to be the exception. The case for a new constitutional settlement – particularly as advanced by Charter '88, on which I shall focus – is in presentation pretentious and in substance flawed. Even if the analysis advanced was a valid one, the prescriptions put forward would not rectify the faults that are identified.

There is, I contend, a case to be made against the Charter and for the existing Constitution. This chapter intends to put that case.

THE CASE FOR A NEW CONSTITUTIONAL SETTLEMENT

What, then, is the argument advanced for a new Constitution? The argument is twofold. First, that the traditional checks and balances in the political system have been eroded, allowing an unchecked Executive to have passed whatever measures of public policy it wishes to have passed. And secondly, that the Executive – especially the present government – has used its now unfettered power to trample the rights of different groups and of the individual in the United Kingdom. As a result, according to Hillyard and Percy-Smith, the coercive state has arrived.[7]

The roots of Executive domination are to be found in the constitutional settlement of 1688–9. The settlement, through the Bill of Rights of 1689, limited the power of one over-mighty Executive (the Crown) but also, by confirming the legal omnipotence of the outputs of Parliament, created the conditions for the emergence of another. If the sovereign could not override the law made by the King-in-Parliament, then neither could his subjects, including the judges. Acts of Parliament could not be set aside other than by Parliament itself. Whosoever controlled Parliament thus enjoyed a mighty power.

What checks existed on this power were, as Dicey recognised in his magisterial work on the subject, checks internal to the political system.[8] Ministers of the Crown were subject to the constraints of the two Houses of Parliament. Furthermore, in the eighteenth and nineteenth centuries such checks were largely unnecessary. The area deemed legitimate for the encroachment of public policy was a narrow one. Few Public General Acts were passed. Only in the late nineteenth century and throughout the twentieth, as government responsibilities have grown and the power of party has overwhelmed the internal constraints, has the potential for an overmighty Executive – encroaching on areas previously considered inviolable – been realised.

The monarchy no longer constitutes a restraint on a determined government. The legislative powers of the House of Lords have been statutorily curtailed. Even what veto power it retains it has lacked the political will to employ. (By agreement between the two front benches, the House does not divide on the Second Reading of measures promised in the government's election manifesto.) In the House of Commons party loyalty dominates. That loyalty is partly the product of political socialisation and partly the product of ambition: those who determine ministerial promotion are the Prime Minister and the party whips. Furthermore, a party-orientated and amateur House has been inadequate to the task of monitoring and restraining a growing executive, an executive prone to secrecy – a particular feature of the twentieth century – and with the might of an experienced and permanent civil service at its disposal. Parliament, in short, has lacked the political will and the resources – intellectual and physical – necessary to act as an effective check on a government determined to get its way.

Power within government, the argument goes, has become more centralised in postwar years. The grip of party has become tighter. By 1965 Samuel Beer was able to declare that party cohesion in the House of Commons was so close to 100 per cent that there was no longer any point in measuring it;[9] a similar degree of party cohesion was noted in the House of Lords.[10] At the apex of government the Prime Minister has utilised the powers of the office – combined with those that flow from the position of party leader – to achieve a greater degree of control over the Cabinet. Richard Crossman in the 1960s warned of the growth of prime ministerial government; Tony Benn echoed his words in the 1970s. 'The present centralisation of power into the hands of one person', he declared, 'has gone too far and amounts to a system of personal rule in the very heart of our parliamentary democracy.[11]

Such perceptions of centralisation have become more acute since 1979. Any doubts harboured by critics as to the existence of highly centralised power in British government were dispelled by the experience of the Thatcher administration. In order to achieve a free market economy, a strong state has had to be crafted.[12] The ramparts of corporatism have been scaled: interest groups were kept at arm's length. The Cabinet was 'handbagged' – kept (as Peter Hennessy noted in Chapter 2) from discussing economic policy for more than a year following the party's return to office and meeting less frequently than its predecessors; critics within the Cabinet were dismissed. The payroll vote in the House of Commons has been enhanced by the increase in the number of Parliamentary Private Secretaries (PPSs), unpaid assistants to ministers who are expected to vote with the government.[13] Opposition parties in the House of Lords, especially the Liberal Democratic Party, have generally been starved of new peers, the creation of 'working peers' not usually keeping pace with the growing infirmity and death of existing peers.

Impediments to the government's policy of limiting public spending have been removed (the Greater London Council and the metropolitan county councils) or subject to statutory limitations (abolition of supplementary rates, rate-capping, community-charge-capping). The longer the government has been in office, the greater the arrogance of power; and the greater the assumption that it will continue to be in office. 'The government', declared Bernard Crick in 1988, 'now habitually changes national institutions as if it assumes… that re-election is as certain as the resurrection of the body after death. In formal terms of political theory the government has become the state.'[14]

There is nothing standing between the individual citizen and the might of the state. Consequently, it is argued, that might has variously been used with impunity to limit or deny the rights and liberties of individual citizens and of particular groups of citizens. Citizens are watched over and constrained by powerful – and secretive – organs of the state. Not only have the ramparts of the corporatist state had to be scaled but so too have those defending the permissive society of earlier decades. The citizen has had to be forced not only to be economically free but also socially responsible. Permissiveness in the past had gone too far. 'If the measures taken to correct this situation happened to invade what liberals of the left chose to think of as civil liberties, that had to be accepted in the interests of the broader goals.'[15] Issues of civil liberty have consequently been to the fore since 1979, with the government taking measures condemned by opposition parties as constraining such liberty: restrictions on freedom of information and expression (a new Official Secrets Act, injunctions against various media, prosecution of serving and former civil servants); extension of police powers (the 1984 Police and Criminal Evidence Act, renewal of the Prevention of Terrorism Act, increase in the size and resources of the police force); restrictions on unpopular minorities such as the trade unions (banning of union membership at GCHQ Cheltenham, limiting the powers of the unions in respect of secondary picketing, unballoted strike action and closed shops) and homosexuals (section 28 of the 1988 Local Government Act); and restrictions on the right to public assembly and peaceful protest (the 1986 Public Order Act). The result, according to Ewing and Gearty, is that 'civil liberties in Britain are in a state of crisis'.[16] Hillyard and Percy-Smith's coercive state is upon us.

Such infringements of civil liberties, it is variously conceded, are not peculiar to the present government. Previous governments tampered with the liberties of the individual.[17] However, the process of infringement – of an erosion of liberty – has gathered momentum since 1979, especially under the government of Margaret Thatcher but with nothing to prevent its continuance under the government of John Major. Relying on the goodwill of ministers is insufficient: action is deemed necessary. That, it is claimed, should take the form of the codification of basic rights in a Bill of Rights and the introduction of more powerful checks and balances in the political system, all to be embodied in a written Constitution. Under the existing unwritten – or to use Nevil Johnson's more accurate term 'unformalised' – Constitution, the rules of the game are not adumbrated and are subject to change by the winning team. What is necessary is a codified set of rules, protected by a neutral umpire (the courts). Hence, the new constitutional settlement proposed by Lord Scarman and by the signatories of Charter '88.

This argument is now well documented with much supporting material. As the attack on civil liberties has, according to Charter '88, gained momentum, so too has the literature claiming to detail it. McAuslan and McEldowney called attention to the dissonance between constitutional theory and practice in the introduction to their edited work *Law, Legitimacy and the Constitution* in 1985. Harden and Lewis took up a similar theme in *The Noble Lie* published the following year. A number of works appeared in the tercentenary year of the Glorious Revolution: Holme and Elliott's *1688–1988: Time for a New Constitution*, Hillyard and Percy-Smith's *The Coercive State*, and Graham and Prosser's *Waiving the Rules*. (The same year, of course, saw the inauguration of Charter '88.) The following year came Thornton's *Decade of Decline: Civil Liberties in the Thatcher Years* and the sixth edition of *Street's Freedom, The Individual and the Law*, edited by Geoffrey Robertson; and in 1990 came Ewing and Gearty's *Freedom Under Thatcher: Civil Liberties in Modern Britain*. The list is illustrative rather than exhaustive. Such works have been variously complemented by journal articles, monographs and newspaper features.

The argument for a new constitutional settlement has clearly to be taken seriously. It is a plausible argument. Not surprisingly, to those whom I have described as the politically dispossessed – those who under the present administration chatter but don't matter – it is a seductive argument. However, it is a flawed argument. It is based on an essentially false thesis; it exaggerates – and to a large extent isolates – developments of the past decade; and it displays the very dissonance which some discern in present constitutional arrangements. The dissonance is between diagnosis and prescription. The medicine prescribed will not cure

the supposed ills; and by generating the impression that it will, proponents of a new constitution are feeding expectations that cannot be met.
As such, their advocacy of a new constitutional settlement is not only
flawed but dangerous.

AN ESSENTIALLY FLAWED THESIS

At the heart of the elective dictatorship thesis is, as we have seen, the
centralisation of power. Power is now centralised – and unfettered. 'The
idea that power is widely dispersed throughout society, with checks and
balances on its exercise, is a fiction. Moreover, the legislature is no
longer able to control the executive, while the judiciary is all too often
prepared to make decisions in support of the powerful.'[18] This statement,
as may be inferred from the preceding section, is a fairly typical
expression of those favouring a new constitutional settlement. It is also
contestable in every particular.

That there has been *some* centralisation of power in central government I do not seek to deny. However, that in itself is not the most
significant feature of power relations in the British polity. What is as, or
more, significant is the extent to which the political system remains
highly pluralist; and, indeed, the extent to which it is, if anything,
fragmenting rather than being cemented at the centre. British government faces forces which are centrifugal rather than centripetal.

Reflecting on the attempts by government to strengthen its position,
Peter Riddell has observed that 'this does not mean that Britain has
become an irreversibly authoritarian society. Pluralism is battered, but
not destroyed'.[19] I would go further in stressing the resilience of pluralism.
Entrenched groups – the big battalions – remain, in some cases battered
but by no means cowed. Indeed, the strength of such groups has been a
marked feature of British society. The legislative outputs of Parliament
may be binding, but various groups have been too well entrenched
economically, politically or socially – enjoying support from powerful
attentive publics or from the general public – for governments to dare
contemplate taking action against them. When the present government
has tried – directing its fire especially at public and private bodies
employing restrictive practices – it has enjoyed significant success only
in respect of a few 'soft' targets, notably the trade unions (declining
membership, dwindling economic leverage, and no great reserves of
popular support) and, to a much, lesser extent, universities and schools

(no economic leverage and – in the case of higher education – little popular or political support), though even here the effect of government policy has been far less than government intended. Measures levelled at local government have been numerous in large part because of the difficulty of actually achieving government goals (see Chapter 5). The divorce between central and local government élites has contributed to the degree of autonomy enjoyed by local government, a position which central government – despite its formal powers – has found it near-impossible to overcome. Central government in Britain still finds it more difficult to impose its will directly at local level than is the case, for instance, with central government in France.

Attempts to reform other well-entrenched bodies, such as the legal profession, have been characterised by the strength of the resistance. As we have seen (Chapters 1 and 3), lawyers in 1989 were able to draw on their not-inconsiderable number in the House of Lords, with the outcome of reform being less than government intended. Even the National Health Service managed to mount a campaign of stiff resistance to proposed reforms, drawing on a large measure of public support often mobilised through the medium of doctors' waiting-rooms and surgeries. And even if some of the larger battalions are formally constrained, those constraints are often difficult to impose at the sharp end of professionally based organisations. Government, for example, is not in a position to second-guess the clinical judgement of surgeons. Ensuring police officers conform to particular rules presents obvious problems. Even ensuring that civil servants and local councils implement statutory requirements is far from problem-free, in part because of the scale of the exercise and in part because of the way in which such requirements may be interpreted.

More significant, though, in the context of this argument, is the growth of the little battalions. There has been a significant growth in the number of pressure groups in recent years. As we have already noted (Chapter 4), one 1979 directory of pressure groups revealed that over 40 per cent of the groups had come into existence since 1960. Such groups have been active in exploiting opportunities for influencing public policy: as we shall see, they have constituted important inputs into both the parliamentary process and the incremental policy-formulation process of Whitehall. Many of the contemporary debates about particular rights – such as the rights of the unborn child versus the right of the woman to choose – revolve around campaigns initiated and sustained by pressure groups, not by government.

Government, then, has to contend with a society which, in terms of organised interests, is more rather than less pluralist. Furthermore, it has to operate in a political environment in which power is more dispersed than before. The most important shift of policy-making power has taken place as a consequence of Britain's membership of the European Community. As a result of membership from 1 January 1973 policy-making competence in certain sectors has passed upward from the British government to the decision-making institutions of the Community. And the power of those bodies has been enhanced considerably by the implementation in 1987 of the Single European Act. As a result of the extension of qualified majority voting in the Council of Ministers, it is now possible – to a greater extent than ever before – for a measure to be approved by the Council and consequently to be enforced as law in the United Kingdom (under the provisions of the 1972 European Communities Act), even though that measure has the approval neither of the British government nor of the British Parliament. Such a situation has already been realised.

British government is not only constrained by the law-making processes of the Council and Commission of the EC but also by the precedence accorded EC law and its interpretation by the EC Court of Justice. The 1972 EC Act not only gave the force of law to all existing and future EC legislation, it also provided that in the event of any conflict between domestic (known as municipal) law and EC law, the provisions of the latter were to prevail. Section 3(1) of the Act provided that any dispute as to the interpretation, effect or validity of the EC treaties, or of any legislation made under them, was to be treated by British judges as a matter of law. Cases which reach the highest domestic court of appeal, the House of Lords, must (under the Rome Treaty) be referred to the Court of Justice for a definitive ruling. (Lower courts may request from the Court a ruling on the interpretation of the treaties.) The effect of these provisions has not been formally to destroy the concept of parliamentary sovereignty – Parliament retains the power to repeal the Acts of 1972 and 1986 and EC law derives its legal force from the provisions of the 1972 Act[20] – but it has been to circumscribe significantly the scope of UK law.

This was variously apparent before 1990, with legislation in the UK on occasion being modified or introduced in order to comply with the rulings of the Court of Justice, but it was not until that year that the extent of the constitutional implications of the Court's power was more fully realised. In June 1990 a number of Spanish fishermen challenged certain nationality provisions of the 1988 Merchant Shipping Act (designed to protect British fishermen's EC quota), claiming that they conflicted with EC law. The Court ruled that, while the case was being heard, they could suspend the application of the provisions of the Act until the outcome was known.[21] In the following month the House of Lords granted an order to the Spanish owners of 53 named vessels restraining the Secretary of State for Transport from 'withholding or withdrawing' their registration in the register of British fishing vessels, the order to remain in force until the Court of Justice had decided the case.

In her Bruges speech in 1988 Mrs Thatcher gave public voice to her fears about the extent of regulation that was now possible from the institutions of the Community. By 1990, with the Council of Ministers variously passing measures against the wishes of the UK government and with the Court of Justice ruling that the provisions of a UK Act of Parliament could be suspended, these fears were more fully realised. Policy-making powers, and consequently the initiative in policy-making, has passed in various sectors to the EC. That is clear from Chapter 6; as Lord Clinton-Davis makes clear, if one is to determine the direction of EC regulation, Brussels is the place to be.

However, policy-making power has not only passed upward from the Cabinet to the institutions of the EC, it has also passed downward. A significant and growing feature of policy-making in the UK in postwar years has been the growth of small, fluid policy communities, comprising the civil servants from the appropriate section of a Department and the representatives of affected outside organisations. They meet in order to discuss and agree policy adjustments. The policy style, as Richardson and Jordan have recorded, is one of accommodation: it is in the interests of both sides to reach agreement, the policy adjustment agreed to then being passed upward in the Department for formal approval.[22] Despite the arm's-length approach adopted by the Thatcher administration towards peak organisations in the formulation of high policy, no such arm's-length approach has been adopted by Departments in the day-to-day process of low- and medium-level policy adjustments. Statutory Instruments remain often the product of extensive consultation.[23] Departmental circulars and other forms of quasi-legislation[24] remain frequently the product of discussion with affected groups, representatives of the groups sometimes being responsible for the drafting. Indeed, the extent of activity by such policy communities is almost certainly greater now than ever before, in part because of the quantitative growth in the number of pressure groups and by the greater qualitative capacity of groups to pinpoint and lobby the relevant officials in Whitehall, now often operating through the medium of professional lobbyists.[25]

Furthermore, the growth of public legislation in volume terms means that the individual ministers and their officials remain important figures in their own right in determining the thrust and content of measures placed before Parliament. For groups seeking to influence the introduction of a particular measure or, more likely, to influence the provisions of a particular measure, the place to head for is the relevant Department. For groups seeking to influence a decision, authority for which is already vested by statute, the person to head for is the individual minister: by virtue of the doctrine of individual ministerial responsibility, statutory powers are vested in individual ministers, not in the government collectively, not in the Cabinet, and not in the Prime Minister. (The Prime Minister and the Cabinet enjoy no statutory powers.) And much will depend on the individual. Nowhere is this better reflected than in the Department of Trade and Industry: the powers vested in the Secretary of State are often broad and vague and their interpretation and use will vary from minister to minister, depending often upon which body has managed to get the minister's ear. The influence will often come from outside, not from above.

The policy-making process, then, is far more complex and fragmented than a simple power-centralisation model would suggest. For those seeking to influence public policy, the policy cycle is a multiple access one; as a result of EC membership, more so now than before. Furthermore, that access has been widened as groups – and individual citizens – have discovered the value of Westminster.

Parliament is not part of the policy-making process. It is a reactive body: it scrutinises and influences measures brought before it. To assert that it 'is no longer able to control the Executive' is contestable on two grounds. First, if by control one means positive direction of public policy, then Parliament has never enjoyed control; therefore, it cannot be something it is 'no longer' able to do. Secondly, if control is taken in the sense of providing the broad limits within which government may govern, of influencing and even restraining measures of public policy, then recent years have witnessed no decline in parliamentary control. Rather, the reverse. The past 20 years have witnessed two significant waves of parliamentary activity: the first, beginning in the 1970s, was a greater degree of backbench independence; the second, beginning in 1979, was the generation of more refined structures for the continuous scrutiny of government – either directly by the House of Commons, primarily through the departmentally related Select Committees appointed in 1979, or through agencies established by Parliament, most notably the National Audit Office.[26] These developments may not be sufficient to create a Parliament able to restrain a government to the extent that critics may wish; but they are sufficient to disprove claims of a marked decline in parliamentary 'control'.

Furthermore, these developments have taken place concomitant with – indeed, may well have encouraged – a greater awareness of Parliament on the part of pressure groups and constituents. It is this awareness that is the focus of Chapter 4. Over the past decade pressure groups have, in effect, discovered Parliament. Lobbying of MPs and peers is now extensive. The better-organised groups have their own in-house lobbyists or employ political consultants; the less-well-organised employ a scatter-gun approach, writing to most or all Members of Parliament. There is no necessarily strong correlation between the wealth of groups and their effectiveness in lobbying: consumer groups are among the groups credited with being especially effective lobbyists.[27] As we have seen (Chapter 4), the input of such groups in the parliamentary process is now significant, not least during the legislative process. By their activity groups have provided Parliament with alternative sources of advice to that of government. As a result of their activities legislation is now subject to not infrequent amendment. And, as Chapter 4 detailed, constituents too now make much greater use of their MPs: an MP on average now receives in one day roughly the amount of mail that in the 1960s he or she used to receive in one week. MPs use their position to ensure that constituency grievances are dealt with at a higher level than could be achieved by the constituent alone and have generally proved successful in achieving the responses sought by constituents. They have also become increasingly active as lobbyists for local and regional interests.[28]

Implicit in this development is the fact that, far from popular participation in political activity having declined, it has actually increased. Avenues of participation have not been closed off. As the British Social Attitudes Surveys of the 1980s discovered, citizens are willing to take action if they deem it necessary (contacting the MP constituting the most popular form of individual action).[29] In practice, most have not done so. However, more have done so in recent years than before and, when they have done so, they have proved willing to employ existing channels. Indeed, the 1986 Social Attitudes Survey detected a 'widespread and growing self-confidence on the part of the electorate to try to bring influence to bear on Parliament'.[30]

As for the courts, judicial independence – as we have seen in Chapter 3 – remains a highly defended principle. There is no significant evidence of erosion. As for the tendency of the courts to side with the interests of the state, there *is* evidence to support this assertion. However, the tendency is not a new one nor – more importantly – is it a growing one. The period since the mid-1960s has witnessed a new judicial activism, with a greater willingness by courts to review ministerial acts. The Labour government in the 1970s lost a number of celebrated cases; the Conservative government has done so since 1979.[31] The fact that the government has lost some cases, combined with the sheer increase in the number of cases of judicial review, has served to impose an important anticipatory constraint on government departments. Since 1981 the number of applications for judicial review has never been less than 500. 'Judicial review of central government decisions', declared *The Economist* in 1989, 'has become so common that all civil servants are now briefed on the dangers of falling foul of the "judge on your shoulder" as one internal Whitehall document puts it.'[32]

A particular government policy and its implementation may thus be subject to parliamentary scrutiny or judicial review (or both) to an extent not previously possible or expected. Action by the courts and Parliament, furthermore, is public action. Though there is clearly a case to be made for more open government, the extent to which the Select Committees of the House of Commons have contributed to prising open departments – and other public agencies – deserves far greater recognition than it has so far been accorded.

The past decade, then, has not witnessed a persistent, exclusive and incontrovertible concentration of power in the hands of the Prime Minister and Cabinet. There has been *some* concentration in *some* areas. However, far more significant has been the fragmentation of power. In so far as there is a predominant new direction in British politics it is this fragmenting of power. It is clearly not an exclusive development – hence, in the title of this volume, 'new directions' – but it deserves to be drawn out and emphasised.

To identify the persistence of pluralism in British politics and a leakage of policy-making power from the apex of government is, by itself, not sufficient to destroy the arguments advanced by proponents of Charter '88. Nor is it to suggest that there are not problems with the form and activity of government, especially particular agencies of government. It is, however, sufficient to undermine the central explanatory premiss on which the Charter is based. On the basic charge levelled against government, there is insufficient evidence to convict.

EXAGGERATION

The power-concentration model is, then, not sustainable. Neither is the claim that there has been a persistent, increasingly extensive and virtually exclusive erosion of individual rights over the past decade.

The underlying historical trend has been one of an extension of rights. Political rights have been variously extended since early in the nineteenth century, most notably but not exclusively through an extension of the franchise. By 1950, following the abolition of the plural vote, the principle of 'one person, one vote' was realised. Since then there has been the extension of the franchise to 18–20-year-olds (1969) and to British citizens living abroad (1985). Social rights, which were restricted rather than extended in the nineteenth century (abortion was made a statutory offence for the first time in 1803, male homosexual relations were outlawed in 1885), have been most significantly extended in recent decades, notably but not exclusively in the latter half of the 1960s.[33] Economic rights – for worker and consumer – have been variously extended, for example through legislation against unfair dismissal, through the growth of an (admittedly *ad hoc*) array of agencies for grievance resolution, and through a growing body of consumer-protection legislation.

It is important to stress that the trend is an underlying one. History is pockmarked with measures – or particular actions – which have in one form or another limited or infringed particular rights. Among some of the best-known measures are those enacted, often hurriedly, at time of perceived threat to the safety of the realm or the maintenance of the King's peace: for example, the 1911 Official Secrets Act, the 1936 Public Order Act and the various emergency provisions of the Second World War, some of which lingered well beyond the conclusion of hostilities. Others have been the consequence of the perceived needs of a growing, more urban and more mobile society: Planning Acts and provision for compulsory purchase, for example. Some of the measures have been temporary; most have remained in force or been superseded by new measures.

Has the underlying trend been reversed since 1979? The claims made by critics in support of this proposition are contestable on several grounds. First, in their marshalling of material to demonstrate that central government has significantly infringed rights and liberties, critics adopt a 'kitchen sink' approach. Everything is thrown in. Making the very mistake for which they criticise the judge, Mr Justice McCowan, in the *Ponting* case (equating the state with the government of the day), critics include actions by agencies of the state which the government did not initiate and did not know about until after the event (police harassment of a particular group, for example, or the shooting of innocent individuals by armed officers); one pair of critics even manage to include the size of the prison population – which government itself is keen to reduce – in the indictment.

Secondly, no recognition is given to those measures which protect or further rights. The provisions of the 1984 Police and Criminal Evidence Act (itself the product of extensive consultations) are often censored for increasing police powers but rarely commended for extending safeguards for suspects in custody; many police officers view the provisions of the Act as a major burden and limitation on their work. The government is attacked for supporting an amendment to the 1988 Local Government Bill prohibiting the intentional promotion of homosexuality by local authorities (introduced under pressure from one source – a number of Conservative backbenchers), while little reference is made to its extension of the provisions of the 1967 Sexual Offences Act to Northern Ireland (introduced under pressure from another source – the European Court of Human Rights). Other measures – such as the Data Protection Act, and the 1989 Security Services Act which creates a statutory framework within which the Security Service has to operate – are criticised for not going far enough; hardly demonstrable proof of an absolute diminution of rights.

Thirdly, evidence is offered largely in a historical vacuum. The obsession with government secrecy is not peculiar to the present government but reflects what Geoffrey Robertson concedes is 'a permanent state of official mind'.[34] Pursuit of 'whistle-blowers' in government, prosecution of those – journalists and civil servants – who put unauthorised information into the public domain, attempts to influence what the media transmit (pressure on the BBC, use of D-Notices), and the deportation of those considered a threat to national security are features of past decades and former governments. The 'state of mind' pervades Labour as well as Conservative governments. This is by no means to excuse, or to seek to explain away, the actions of government but is rather to put the problem in context.

All this does not demonstrate that there is no problem with secrecy and the protection of civil rights in this country. What it does challenge, though, is the assertion that we have witnessed some paradigmatic change since 1979: that there has been a deliberate attack on the rights and liberties of the individual that stands in marked contrast to anything that has gone before and that this has been the consequence of a power-centralising government. The picture is not that simple. It rarely is.

Any pressure for the greater protection of rights starts from a strong, not a collapsed or collapsing, base. Paul Sieghart, the Chairman of the European Human Rights Foundation, has argued for the greater protection of human rights in the UK but in so doing has conceded that 'judged by any objective measure, human rights and fundamental freedoms are better respected in the UK today than they are in the great majority of the world's other countries. Quite where at the top of the league table she stands may be debatable, but it must certainly be somewhere in the top ten, if not the top five. Given her history, that is hardly surprising, and it is also very creditable.'[35] Such observations are not grounds for complacency – there is no reason why Britain should not strive for first position in the league table – but they do put in perspective the contemporary position in the United Kingdom, and in so doing provide an important backdrop for any discussion of a new constitutional settlement, including a Bill of Rights, for the UK.

DISSONANCE

The final argument that can be deployed against proponents of a new constitutional settlement – by far the most compelling argument – is that their proposed remedies will not solve the ailments they claim to diagnose.

The proposed 'cure' for the ailment of an over-mighty government bent on curtailing the rights of the individual is a package of measures designed to limit the powers of government and (as part of the package) a Bill of Rights embodying the basic human rights of the citizen. Utilising a Bill of Rights to deal with various of the problems identified by civil libertarians is a blunt and potentially ineffective tool; and limiting central government may actually exacerbate rather than solve the problem.

Bills of Right or their equivalent, such as the European Convention on Human Rights, are by their nature broad documents. They are, in essence, basic statements designed to endure; hence, they are couched in general rather than specific terms. And given that the community itself is recognised as having rights in relation to the individual – such as the right to deprive a person of liberty if that person is found guilty of committing murder or grievous assault – they embody qualifications and derogations. The European Convention on Human Rights, for example, declares that no restrictions shall be placed on the rights it enumerates 'other than such as are prescribed by law and are necessary in a democratic society in the interests of national security or public safety'. The first three articles of Title I of the Italian Constitution list rights which are declared 'inviolable', each followed by an immediate qualification. To take the shortest example: 'The liberty and secrecy of correspondence and of every form of communication are', under the third article, 'inviolable.' This is followed immediately by: 'Limitations upon them may only be enforced by a warrant issued by a judicial authority in accordance with the guarantees laid down by law.' The 'inviolable' rights of personal liberty and personal domicile are subject to similar qualification. The Greek Constitution is not dissimilar. According to Article 3, 'Personal liberty is inviolable. No one shall be prosecuted, arrested, imprisoned or otherwise confined except when and as the law provides.' An earlier Article confers the right of citizens to develop freely their personalities and participate in the social, economic and political life of the country, 'in so far as they do not infringe upon the rights of others or violate the Constitution and *moral values*' (my emphasis).

Constitutional statements of right, then, are usually general and qualified. The more general they are, the greater the power vested in those whose task it is to interpret their provisions. It is not axiomatic that it is the courts, but they are the authority normally given the task. As we have already observed, the courts in Britain are not necessarily viewed by critics as the best defenders of individual rights, and the qualifications introduced would normally allow a government broad scope for restrictive measures. The essential value of a Bill of Rights is as a general guiding authority in a new state or in one that has to start afresh in crafting a Constitution or form of government: the USA, 'the first new nation' in Seymour Martin Lipset's phrase, offers the first example, and in Europe – prior to events of 1989–90 – Greece offers the most recent. It has less obvious applicability in an established polity with a body of rights established by statute and common law and with well-established norms, including judicial independence.

Bills of Right, then, are rarely well-honed tools for protecting specific rights. Incorporating the European Convention on Human Rights into British law would certainly not offer the quantum leap forward in the protection of rights that proponents appear to imply. The United Kingdom is already a signatory to the convention and the advantage of incorporation, as a former Home Secretary who favours incorporation has conceded, would be one principally of convenience.[36] Generating a tailor-made Bill of Rights for the United Kingdom would be fraught with difficulty. The more detailed the measure, the less likelihood there is of achieving consensus in support of its provisions. The more general it is, the greater the interpretative power of the courts.

Evidence culled from abroad points to the limitations. Homosexuals in the United States, for example, have found that they enjoy no protection under the US Constitution. The US Supreme Court has discovered a right to privacy in the 'penumbra' of the provisions of the constitution, but it has not found that such a right encompasses homosexual relations conducted in private. Consequently, in some states of the USA homosexual conduct between consenting adults is a criminal offence while it is not an offence in the UK. What protection is afforded to gays in the USA has been through statute. (A 1990 federal statute aimed at 'hate crimes' was the first to include explicit reference to homosexuals.) And what protection the Constitution has afforded ethnic minorities has been sporadic, measures to ensure the exercise of effective civil rights being enacted by statute (such as the 1964 Civil Rights Act and the 1965 Voting Rights Act). Those measures had to be taken to overcome the effect of another element of the US constitutional structure – federalism. (As Duane Lockard has noted, federalism in the USA has been the greatest protector of racism.[37]) The USA stands as an exemplar of a system with an entrenched Bill of Rights and institutionalised checks and balances. It also demonstrates that a Bill of Rights is not necessarily an automatic guarantor of rights claimed by different groups in society.

It does not follow, then, that a UK Bill of Rights would necessarily provide a redress of the grievances delineated in recent critiques of civil liberties in Britain. Indeed, if one takes many of the complaints levelled by critics and place those criticisms alongside the constitutional protection afforded to rights in other countries, it is by no means apparent that a Bill of Rights would offer a significant remedy. Restrictive provisions on nationality and immigration are not peculiar to the UK, neither are instances of harassment and excessive behaviour by police and other public agencies. Indeed, if one takes the string of measures offered by Hillyard and Percy-Smith as helping collectively to create the coercive state – the creation of housing action trusts and urban development corporations; the national curriculum in schools; the primacy accorded to Christianity in religious education in schools; section 28 of the 1988 Local Government Act; the 1990 Official Secrets Act and attempts to ensure secrecy; attempts at media censorship; the accumulation of personal data by the Department of Social Security; the reduction in the number of long-stay institutions for the physically and mentally ill; the increase in the size (and 'militarisation') of the police force; the extension of police powers and the Prevention of Terrorism Act[38] – it is likely that only a very few would be affected significantly by the provisions of a Bill of Rights, however narrowly or widely drawn. If the steamroller of the coercive state is upon us a Bill of Rights is far from likely to offer an effective brake.

Nor is it likely to offer the educative tool that proponents suggest: that is, by having a Bill of Rights the citizen knows precisely what his or her rights are and can then act to protect them if they are infringed. The problem with this is that such measures afford no such certainty. Judicial interpretation can change in a relatively short space of time and, indeed, can offer uncertainty rather than precision. The US Supreme Court offers a daunting example, rights under the constitution being determined on occasion by the swing vote of one Justice or being left unclear because of a failure to reach agreement; the fields of obscenity and capital punishment are particular legal quagmires. Furthermore, even if rights are enumerated, there is no guarantee that the average citizen will have the resources necessary to pursue remedial action in cases of infringement.

A Bill of Rights, then, is not necessarily the valuable weapon in the armoury of constitutional reform that Chartists believe it to be. Neither are the other radical proposals they espouse. Electoral reform may offer weak government which, in itself, is not necessarily desirable for the protection of rights and liberties: strong monitoring and, if necessary, control from the centre may be required to keep the security services and the police within acceptable bounds. Nor is electoral reform uncontrovertibly a 'fairer' system than the existing one. It can effect a shift of disproportionate political power from the largest minority party in the country – that enjoying plurality if not majority support – to one enjoying least support.[39] It can also potentially exclude from power a second party for a continuous period of time – longer than that experienced so far by the Labour Party in the UK – and, if generating post-election bargaining to produce a government, may result in an administration enjoying less definitive support in electoral terms than under the present first-past-the-post system.[40] Such bargaining may also produce periods of uncertainty. Uncertainty threatens the effectiveness of government and, if prolonged, that lack of effectiveness threatens popular consent for the system of government itself. Though there is popular support for a 'fairer' system of voting that support drops away markedly if the alternative is one in which no party enjoys an overall majority of seats following a General Election.[41] That the effects of proportional representation are not uniformly beneficial is reflected in the fact that a number of countries with PR systems are experiencing pressure to move away from such systems: notably Israel and Italy.

Nor is devolution of powers to elected national assemblies in Scotland and Wales, and to regional assemblies in England, demonstrably an unquestioned benefit. The more power that is devolved the greater the opportunity to encourage and maintain regional disparities in wealth and also the potential to formalise and enforce local prejudices.[42] Potential for such local prejudice exists presently on a small scale – for example, through the discretion vested in magistrates to interpret certain statutory provisions (as, under the 1986 Public Order Act, to determine whether particular conduct is 'abusive' or 'insulting') – and, depending on what legislative powers are devolved, could emerge on a much larger and contentious scale under regional government. Devolving power to elected assemblies can be justified in terms of democratic theory (whether in practice greater participation would result is another matter); it is not necessarily one that can be justified as liberal or economically progressive. Evidence of the extent to which devolution of power can prove an illiberal measure is present within the history of the United Kingdom of Great Britain and Northern Ireland. The experience of Northern Ireland is exceptional, but sufficient to justify further reflection.

Other proposals also raise considerable questions, in part because of their vagueness and in part because of their potential to inject not balance but stalemate into the political system. A 'democratic' (meaning presumably elected) second chamber offers the potential for challenge to the elected first chamber; as for the powers that such an elected body would have the Charter is silent. Placing the executive 'under the power of a democratically renewed Parliament' raises far more questions than it answers. How is it to be placed 'under the power' of Parliament? Is

Parliament to exercise power on a scale similar to that of, say, the United States Congress? If so, the potential for government being denied the power to govern – that is, to prepare a coherent programme and proceed on the basis of likely but not guaranteed assent by Parliament – is great; and, if realised, threatens to undermine consent in a political culture more geared to the dictum of 'the government must govern' than that of the United States. And if the power is not to be so great, what form is it to take? As for placing all agencies of the state under the rule of law, the essential problem here is one of definition. What, precisely, is 'the rule of law'? According to Dicey, it is one of the two pillars of the British Constitution. However, the term is employed to mean very different things – sometimes to mean procedural rights, sometimes to refer to the common application of law[43] – and it is far from clear what is entailed by the term in the context of the Charter. It sounds a fine principle, one to which all can subscribe, but the reason why all can subscribe is because it means different things to those subscribing.

As for the overall package of measures, all to be embodied in a written Constitution, it falls foul of two major criticisms: one is that it is unachievable; the other, related but separable, is that it is dangerous and can actually be harmful to achieving recognition and protection of the rights of the individual.

The proposal for a written Constitution is unachievable because no formal means exist for its enactment. The same applies to an entrenched Bill of Rights. Under the existing Constitution there is no way in which Parliament can rid itself of its omnicompetence. The package of measures embodied in Charter '88 – even shorn of the proposal for a written Constitution – is also unachievable on practical and political grounds. Putting the general statements of principle into concrete form would be time-consuming and achieving a political consensus in order to agree and pass the measures, as a package of measures, a mammoth undertaking. In order to achieve parliamentary approval the parties would have to agree that such a time-consuming, fundamental reform should have priority over everything else. The prospects for that are bleak. The Conservative Party is an opponent of radical constitutional surgery. The Labour leader, Neil Kinnock, has made clear that his party's proposal to reform the House of Lords would not be carried through in the lifetime of the first Parliament of a Labour government. And even if there were to be cross-party agreement among leaders, there is no guarantee – as past experience on Lords' reform and devolution has demonstrated – that the leaders would be able to carry their backbenchers with them.

Even were the reforms to be implemented they would not achieve the desired goals. There appears to have been little sustained enquiry undertaken of the precise likely effect of the measures proposed, and little if any of the effect if the constitutional package *as a whole* was implemented. The Chartists appear to proceed on the basis that the measures are desirable in principle. As a result, great effort and resources have been poured in to advocating a new constitutional settlement that may sound attractive but which, in practice, will not have the impact intended. By raising hopes that cannot be met, the Charter is dangerous: it raises the prospect for a collapse of confidence under such a new Constitution and, more immediately, it diverts energy and resources away from tackling present and specific problems, among them a number of constitutional problems on which the Charter is silent, including – as John Lloyd has noted – Northern Ireland, 'which is, after all, where people still die weekly over a constitutional dispute'.[44]

The extent to which the Charter rests on unsure foundations is partially hidden by the portentous – and pretentious – language in which it is couched. The choice of title is influenced by Charter '77 and was adopted in part 'to salute the courage of those in Eastern Europe who still fight for their fundamental freedoms'. Such pretentiousness has endeared it neither to its opponents (predictably enough) nor, in some cases, to its potential friends. Reflecting in 1990 as to why he had been cool towards Charter '88, columnist Peter Jenkins observed that 'it was... obnoxious that ageing, wellheeled, Oxbridge revolutionists should set themselves up on all fours with the brave struggle of the dissidents of Czechoslovakia and take it upon themselves to lecture fully paid-up liberals on the merits of constitutional reform'.[45] Dangerous, then, and pretentious.

So much for the Charter. If the proposals it embodies cannot solve present problems what is to be done? Should those who seek to protect the rights of individuals and groups in society – who seek to raise the UK from somewhere in the top ten to first place in the league table – just pack up and go home? Not at all. The answer is to be found within the present system and the approach to be adopted is twofold.

First, at the level of the political process itself, the answer is to strengthen those institutions able to hold government to account. That means, principally, Parliament. Giving Parliament some new 'power to control government' (presumably over and above the considerable formal power it has already) is dangerous, for reasons already touched upon: it offers the opportunity for stalemate. However, strengthening the institution as a body for scrutinising and influencing government is both desirable and achievable. Recent years have witnessed some of the changes that are possible. There is much more that can be done. As both Fred Silvester and Robert Kilroy-Silk have argued, if Parliament is still not strong enough to defend particular rights, then that is an argument for strengthening Parliament and not for relying on a judge-protected Bill of generalised rights.[46]

Secondly, the answer is to be found in pressing for measures to protect specific rights and to correct demonstrable excesses. In other words, one should focus on proven problems and seek a legislative remedy. This allows not only a concentration of resources, principally lobbying resources, where they are most needed, it also offers a specific means for dealing with a problem. To take a specific example: gays and civil rights activists oppose section 28 of the 1988 Local Government Act especially on the grounds that it has contributed to a climate of oppression; it sends out encouraging signals to those who are only too happy to discriminate against homosexuals and makes local authorities reluctant to provide facilities for gay groups of any sort. They want to see a ban on discrimination. Peter Tatchell has encouraged gays to support Charter '88 on the grounds that protection will be provided through a written Constitution and a Bill of Rights. As we have seen, that is by no means certain. (And certainly not if one were to take Tatchell's sloppy use of language seriously. 'With a democratic constitution', he writes, 'laws that discriminate against lesbians and gay men would be illegal'. Under a liberal constitution, possibly; under a 'democratic' constitution, very doubtful.) In the same issue of the magazine in which Tatchell's Charter '88 endorsement appears, there is carried also the text of a Homosexual Equality Bill, drafted by the legal officer of Justice, Peter Ashman. As Ashman notes, the potential is greater to fight – and win – one parliamentary battle than to fight and win an all-out war.[47] A lobbying group has been formed (the Stonewall Group) and, even if the Bill is not enacted, a lobbying campaign raises the specific problem in a way that generalised support for a Bill of Rights cannot.

There is a related point. Specific measures have a much greater impact on the behaviour of citizens than generalised statements of right. A measure outlawing particular behaviour – such as incitement to racial hatred – will be complied with because it is clear (or usually reasonably clear) what is required, whereas a more generalised statement may not induce compliance because people have no idea what it entails until such time as specific interpretation is given by the courts.

More importantly, a Bill of Rights might even serve to deny those very rights which reformers seek. An absolute freedom of expression, for example, would probably nullify legislation forbidding incitement to racial hatred (in the USA neo-Nazis have been able to use the provisions of the Constitution to great effect); an absolute freedom of the press would allow journalists to indulge in those very excesses – such as invading intensive-care wards to interview accident victims – which are currently being addressed under threat of legislation. No right is absolute unto itself and legislation offers a more precise and flexible tool for determining the dividing line between competing rights. Legislation also offers the opportunity to extend existing rights to meet changing conditions. Thus, for example, existing legislation banning incitement to racial hatred has recently been widened – to encompass the intention to create racial hatred – and extended to cover films, video recordings and other media. There is much to be said for utilising the existing procedures.

A written constitution and a Bill of Rights may sound attractive. The practical reality is that they do not offer what proponents believe they offer. The most effective route for dealing with specific problems is the legislative process. Legislation is the remedy for proven abuses. Concentrating on abuses maximises the potential to rally a consensus behind change. Arguing the case for generalised radical surgery, with unknown consequences, does not. The former entails hard work. If abuses are to be remedied, it entails the chattering classes doing more than raising their pens and reaching for the cheque book.

NOTES

1. A good example of American literature drawing on British experience in the 1950s is J. Macgregor Burns, *The Deadlock of Democracy* (Englewood Cliffs, N.J.: Prentice-Hall, 1963).
2. Lord Hailsham, *Elective Dictatorship* (London: British Broadcasting Corporation, 1976). But see Lord Hailsham, *A Sparrow's Flight: Memoirs* (London: Collins, 1990) pp. 391–6, for a later qualification.
3. Sir K. Joseph, *Freedom Under the Law* (London: Conservative Political Centre, 1975) pp. 11–12.
4. *The Times*, 11 July 1990.
5. Support for some measures of reform – such as more open government – extends beyond the 'wets'. On the groupings within the parliamentary party and their dispositions see P. Norton, ' "The Lady's Not for Turning": But What About the Rest? Margaret Thatcher and the Conservative Party, 1979–1989', *Parliamentary Affairs*, 43 (1), January 1990, pp. 41–58, and 'Choosing a Leader: Margaret

Thatcher and the Parliamentary Conservative Party 1989–90', *Parliamentary Affairs*, 43 (3), July 1990, pp. 249–59.
6. R. B. McDowell, *British Conservatism, 1832–1914* (London: Greenwood Press, 1974) p. 142.
7. P. Hillyard and J. Percy-Smith, *The Coercive State: The Decline of Democracy in Britain* (London: Fontana, 1988).
8. A. V. Dicey, *An Introduction to the Study of the Law of the Constitution* (1885), 10th edn (London: Macmillan, 1959).
9. S. H. Beer, *Modern British Politics*, rev. edn (London: Faber & Faber, 1969) p. 350.
10. P. Bromhead, *The House of Lords and Contemporary Politics, 1911–57* (London: Routledge & Kegan Paul, 1958) p. 118.
11. T. Benn, 'The Case for a Constitutional Premiership', *Parliamentary Affairs*, 33 (1), Winter 1980, p. 7.
12. See especially A. Gamble, *The Free Economy and the Strong State* (London: Macmillan, 1988).
13. See J. Critchley, 'Hidden Dangers of the Payroll Vote', *The Times*, 19 July 1990. See also P. Norton, 'The Constitutional Position of Parliamentary Private Secretaries', *Public Law*, Summer 1989, pp. 232–6.
14. B. Crick, 'Killed by the Facts', *The Guardian*, 14 November 1988.
15. V. Bogdanor, 'The Constitution', in D. Kavanagh and A. Seldon (eds), *The Thatcher Effect* (Oxford: Oxford University Press, 1989) p. 136.
16. K. D. Ewing and C. A. Gearty, *Freedom Under Thatcher* (Oxford: Oxford University Press, 1990) p. 255.
17. Ibid., p. v. See also G. Robertson, *Freedom, The Individual and the Law*, 6th edn (London: Penguin Books, 1989).
18. P. Hillyard and J. Percy-Smith, 'The Coercive State Revisited', *Parliamentary Affairs*, 42 (4), October 1989, p. 546.
19. P. Riddell, *The Thatcher Decade* (Oxford: Blackwell, 1989) p. 183.
20. A repeal of the Acts – in effect, taking the UK out of the Community – would be a breach of the treaties, under which membership is in perpetuity. However, under the doctrine of parliamentary sovereignty the British courts would be expected to enforce the Acts of repeal.
21. *The Financial Times*, 20 June 1990.
22. A. G. Jordan and J. J. Richardson, 'The British Policy Style or the Logic of Negotiation?', in J. J. Richardson (ed.), *Policy Styles in Western Europe* (London: George Allen & Unwin, 1982) pp. 82–4.
23. See P. Norton, 'Public Legislation', in M. Rush (ed.), *Parliament and Pressure Politics* (Oxford: Oxford University Press, 1990) pp. 204–8.
24. See G. Ganz, *Quasi-Legislation* (London: Sweet & Maxwell, 1987).
25. See C. Miller, *Lobbying Government* (Oxford: Blackwell, 1987), and Table 3.1 in C. Grantham and C. Seymour-Ure, 'Political Consultants', in Rush (ed.), *Parliament and Pressure Politics*, pp. 50–6, identifying some of the principal clients of lobbying firms.
26. The developments are summarised in P. Norton, *Parliament in Perspective* (Hull: Hull University Press, 1987). On behavioural changes, see P. Norton, 'The House of Commons: Behavioural Changes', in P. Norton (ed.), *Parliament in the 1980s* (Oxford: Blackwell, 1985) pp. 22–47. On the Select Committees, see G. Drewry (ed.), *The New Select Committees*, 2nd edn (Oxford: Oxford University Press, 1989).
27. Norton, 'Public Legislation', pp. 195–6.
28. See D. Wood, 'The Conservative Member of Parliament as Lobbyist for Constituency Economic Interests', *Political Studies*, 35 (3), September 1987, pp. 393–409.

29. R. Jowell, S. Witherspoon and L. Brook, *British Social Attitudes: The 1987 Report* (Aldershot: Gower, 1987) p. 56.
30. Ibid., p. 58.
31. See the summary in P. Norton, 'The Judiciary', in B. Jones *et al.*, *Politics U.K.* (Oxford: Philip Allan, 1991).
32. *The Economist*, 18 November 1989.
33. See P. G. Richards, *Parliament and Conscience* (London: George Allen & Unwin, 1970).
34. Robertson, *Freedom, the Individual and the Law*, p. 137.
35. P. Sieghart (ed.), *Human Rights in the United Kingdom* (London: Pinter, 1988) p. 4.
36. The Rt. Hon. (now Sir) Leon Brittan, speaking at a Policy Studies Institute seminar, December 1988. See L. Brittan, *Discussions on Policy* (London: Policy Studies Institute, 1989) p. 73.
37. D. Lockard, *The Perverted Priorities of American Politics*, 2nd edn (New York: Macmillan 1976) ch. 4.
38. Hillyard and Percy-Smith, 'The Coercive State Revisited', pp. 533–47.
39. See especially J. Chandler, 'The Plurality Vote: a Reappraisal', *Political Studies*, 30 (1), March 1982, pp. 87–94.
40. Norton, *Parliament in the 1980s*, pp. 148–9.
41. 'The Voters Don't Care for Balance', *The Economist*, 5 July 1986.
42. On the arguments against, see P. Norton, *The Constitution in Flux* (Oxford: Martin Robertson, 1982) ch. 9.
43. Ibid., pp. 15–16, and P. Norton, '"Law and Order" in Perspective', *Contemporary Review*, 251 (no. 1460), September 1987, p. 115.
44. J. Lloyd, 'A Sound Constitution to Keep the Red Flag Flying', *Sunday Correspondent*, 15 July 1990.
45. P. Jenkins, 'Bill of Rights for Labour', *Independent*, 12 July 1990.
46. R. Kilroy-Silk, 'Wrongs of a Bill of Rights', *The Guardian*, 4 February 1977.
47. *Gay Times*, July 1990, pp. 18–19.

Name Index

Subject Index